Revitalizing Japan: Architecture, Urbanization, and Degrowth

A publication of the Japan Research Initiative, Harvard University Graduate School of Design

Revitalizing Japan: Architecture, Urbanization, and Degrowth

Mohsen Mostafavi and
Kayoko Ota, eds.

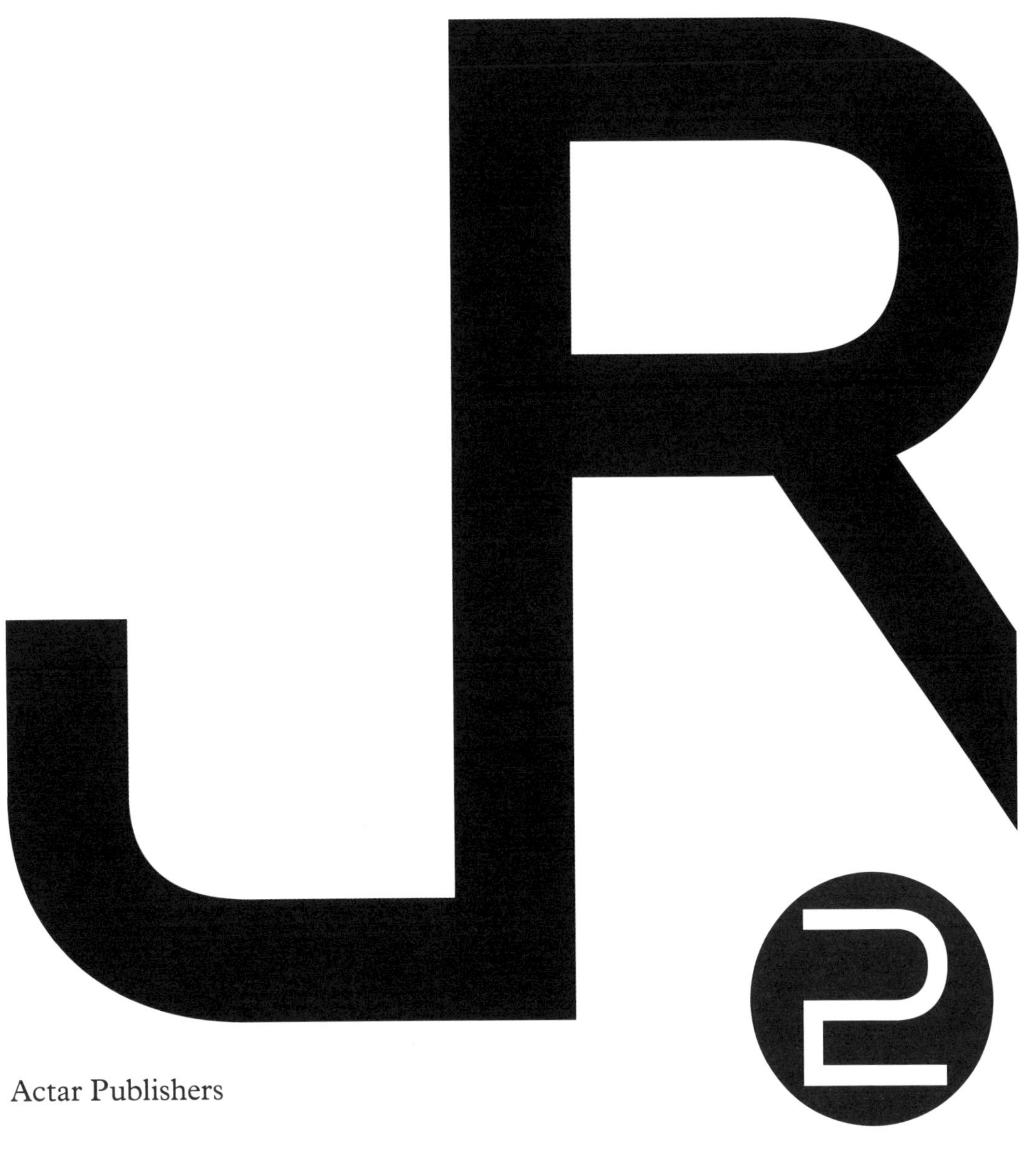

Actar Publishers

CONTENTS

Japan and the Logic of Local Revitalization

Mohsen Mostafavi

Japanese society, so rich and distinct culturally, is also becoming unique demographically. Added to a low birth rate and an aging population—traits shared by many other nations—it has to contend with internal migration and a relatively low rate of immigration by foreigners. Together, these are producing rapid depopulation and shrinking cities.

Some important aspects of Japan's demography can be revealed by the statistics. In 2021, nearly one-third of the population was 65 and older; life expectancy is about 85 years. The fertility rate (TFR) is 1.30 births per woman (2021), and the population of roughly 125 million is decreasing at an annual rate of -0.5%, or approx. 500,000 people a year. The number of foreigners in Japan, including the Chinese, Vietnamese, and Korean workforce, increased to just over three million after COVID. These figures can vary dramatically from region to region. The TFR for major metropolitan areas such as Nagoya, Osaka, and Tokyo can be much lower, with fewer practical incentives and resources for young people to have children. Yet those areas have not suffered from a decrease in population due to local migration.

Many other countries have experienced a dramatic decline in birth rate since the 1960s: China's TFR decreased from a staggering high of 7.51 in 1963 to roughly 1.28 in 2020. But Japan's size and economic structure have given rise to a more noticeable state of disequilibrium between the major cities, which attract young people for education and work, and the regions, which have become the visible sites of demographic change. The disequilibrium between cities and regions, sometimes referred to as the "pole society," describes the simultaneous increase in the population of metropolitan areas and the decrease in the regions.[1]

The depopulation of local regions is invariably accompanied by the abandonment of buildings and the challenge of providing basic resources, including health, education, and transportation. The reduction in this type of necessary infrastructure places further burdens on local communities, with the young migrating to larger cities in search of opportunity and leaving behind an increasingly elderly population in greater need of support such as hospitals and care homes. In addition to shrinking cities, demographic change has resulted in significant changes in the character and formation of the built environment, and if left unattended, this will have serious consequences for the country's regions, further exacerbating the differences in the quality of life between big cities and small communities.

This book is dedicated to addressing the spatial consequences and opportunities of Japan's demographic changes at the regional level. How can the process of revitalizing such areas not only slow the tide of migration to big cities, but also enhance the standard of living of the residents of these areas while attracting migrants and tourists? Still, the topic of local migration is not without its challenges. One of the underlying assumptions in this study is the potential value of more distributed or multi-nodal patterns of migration.

In addition to the challenges of demographic change, Japan has also been occasionally hit by natural disasters, one of the most recent of which was the earthquake and tsunami that affected the Tohoku region in 2011. The lessons of community rebuilding and revitalization following environmental disasters often overlap with those brought about by demographic change. At times, too, these changes share similarities with the economic and spatial consequences of globalization, resulting in the decentralization of regional cities.

The Japanese government, in collaboration with other entities, activists, planners, and architects, has tried to find new ways to respond to the physical emptying out of smaller cities through attempts at rethinking and reconfiguring their urban cores. The government and the railway companies, for example, have undertaken the improvement of the transport infrastructure

1 See, for example, Hisakazu Kato, "Declining Population and the Revitalization of Local Regions in Japan," *Meiji Journal of Political Science and Economics* 3 (2014): 25–35. Kato also links the low birth rate in metropolitan areas to the relative lack of resources for bringing up children (childcare facilities, etc.), which make those harder environments in which to raise children.

of several regional cities. These efforts are often intended to create more compact spatial clusters that will build a network of connections between local communities.

The Tokyo-based office of Kumiko Inui has recently realized two such regional projects; one is a railway station development in Nobeoka in Miyazaki Prefecture, the other a ferry port known as the Miyajimaguchi Passenger Terminal, located to the west of Hiroshima. The redevelopment of the area adjacent to the railway station is planned not only to improve the experience of travel, but also to transform the station into a "porous" urban hub for the city, encouraging connections between the structure's inside and outside. In a city of roughly 114,000 inhabitants, where most of the buildings date from after the end of World War II—Nobeoka was firebombed by the Allied Forces in 1945—the railway station at once creates an urban space and a public building with a variety of facilities for the user. Equally important is the way the station is connected to the existing urban tissue. The result is as much a social undertaking as it is an infrastructural one. The project exemplifies the value of architecture as an urban endeavor.

• • •

The idea of architecture as urbanism and as a social act defines one of the prerequisites for responding to the changes in the urban dynamics of the Japanese regional city. It also characterizes one of the key aspirations of many of the projects featured in this publication. During an earlier period of post-WWII architectural exploration in Japan, architects including Kenzo Tange and members of the Metabolist group were preoccupied with addressing the questions of housing and metropolitan life, often in the context of land scarcity. Their ideas were invariably represented by megastructures, massive pieces of architecture and infrastructure that, through their size and incorporation of a multiplicity of urban functions, nearly ingested the city in the process.

Today, the scale and characteristics of local towns require a different sensibility and an architecture which, like acupuncture, is linked to the pressure points of the city. This type of relational urbanism shares some of its qualities with one of the exceptions to the well-known Metabolist projects, namely the concept of "group form" by Fumihiko Maki and Masato Otaka. The idea is described in Maki's 1964 text, "Investigations in Collective Form," and realized in his iterative and multi-phased urban design for the Hillside Terrace development in Tokyo.[2] The physical demands of Japan's smaller towns also parallel those of a much earlier period, early sixteenth-century Rome as reflected by Michelangelo, among others, in the concept of *renovatio urbis* (urban renovation), or "healing" the city by carefully adding a series of significant urban fragments.

This concept of "healing" may arguably be seen in the works of a small group of architects, including Kumiko Inui, Sou Fujimoto, and Akihisa Hirata, who were brought together in 2011 by Toyo Ito. Their mission was to build a communal meeting house known as "Home for All" in Rikuzentakata in Iwate Prefecture in the aftermath of the Tohoku earthquake. The project is in an area north of the city of Sendai, where Ito's Mediatheque, which was also damaged by the earthquake, is located. On the one hand, the small multistory building, simply constructed, was intended to function as a pavilion and a witness overlooking the devastated landscape; on the other, it provided a place for those who had lost their homes to come together in a series of communal living rooms with outdoor decks.

The iconic images of the structure underscore the importance of the project's symbolic value. More than any other project in Japan in the past ten years, "Home for All," both despite and because of its incredible simplicity, has come to represent the importance of the interconnections between design and society—a marker of the disaster and a sign of hope for the community. As an architect, Toyo Ito has long been at the center of many significant ideas and investigations that address the urban realm. But since Tohoku, a significant part of his work has focused more on regional rather than urban issues. Part of this shift can be attributed to the difficulties facing any architect in Japan today who seeks to have a significant impact on the urban landscape of a city like Tokyo. Still, the experience of working in the disaster-struck region provided him with the opportunity for closer collaboration with a younger generation of architects, as well as the local community.

Prior to the tsunami, Ito had already been engaged with a couple of projects on an island called Omishima in the Seto Inland Sea. The Toyo Ito Museum of Architecture, Imabari (2011), is housed in the Steel Hut and the Silver Hut. The latter was originally Ito's own house in Tokyo, but was moved to Omishima. The museum is dedicated to Ito's work, but also addresses regional issues. For several years, Toyo Ito conducted a series of design studios focused on Omishima at the Harvard Graduate School of Design. Unlike other islands in the Seto Inland Sea that are linked to art and tourism, for Ito, Omishima has provided a valuable opportunity to consider the potentials of local migration through agricultural production.

Following these and other initiatives linked to regional development, there is now an increasing level of activity in Omishima by a younger group of activists and designers. Many have focused their energies on enabling local communities to have more direct involvement with shaping the places where they live and work. This type of individual and community engagement also reduces the reliance of communities on administrative bodies, while at the

2 The original draft of the text was written by Maki as a paper with the title "Some Thoughts on Collective Form," with an introduction to "group form," in January 1961.

same time increasing their potential influence on and input into administrative decision-making.

• • •

This book begins with Toyo Ito's reflections on contemporary Japanese urbanization. Ito believes in the importance of regional cities as the future site of public architecture. He argues that because of increasing costs for local municipal authorities, such architecture has become contingent on the inclusion of two or more functions, and that this type of hybridity will help shape the resultant architecture's distinct characteristics. Hence the need for the younger generation of architects to look to regional cities as sites of innovation.

The main section of the book showcases a series of ideas and practices by a diverse range of contributors interested in regional cities and their potential, including Jun Aoki and Kumiko Inui, who worked in Aoki's office during the early part of her career. Both expand on the themes facing contemporary Japanese urbanization and discuss a few of their own projects. In the remaining essays, a young group of architects and designers address a wide array of relevant topics ranging from questions of representation to fabrication and from economic and social concerns to those of community design, ecology, and the environment.

In the spring of 2023, a group of students from the Harvard Graduate School of Design traveled to Onomichi, a port town on the western side of Japan, in order to conduct a research-based design studio. Onomichi is a typical small town with all the demographic challenges currently facing Japan. The aim of the studio was to find alternative programs and imaginative ways to respond to the conditions facing the city. A key aspect of the studio relies on the potential impact and the simultaneous realization of projects with the aim of densifying and enlivening the city. A small selection of these projects is included in this publication.

The book also presents a selection of images of the city of Onomichi by the photographer Kenta Hasegawa. Hasegawa is one of Japan's most talented photographers, with a wonderful eye for detail. But equally important is the way he has captured the typical qualities of the city to give us a sense of the everyday. The photographs show both urban vistas and close-up images of the city's specific features and particularities. Akin to the work of an ethnographer, Hasegawa's photographs provide a form of visual micro-history. The combination of the photographs and projects from the design studio shows the city as it is and as it might be in the future.

• • •

Revitalizing Japan: Architecture, Urbanization, and Degrowth is, in many ways, also a book about post-growth or "de-growth" society. What happens when growth can no longer be considered the primary engine for societal transformation and contributing to better lives? The challenges of demographic change, not only in Japan but increasingly in other parts of the world, go hand in hand with a planet that is facing the reality of limited resources. This combination demands a new approach to the future of urbanization, one that is both more aware of and responsive to the future ecology of the planet as well as the inequities facing its inhabitants. In this context, it is not surprising to learn that a recent book on Karl Marx and the ecological crisis by Kohei Saito, a young Japanese economist, has sold more than half a million copies. Despite its occasionally controversial reception, Saito's work on "de-growth communism" has clearly hit a nerve in the country and raised the level of debate between the social and the ecological.[3]

The intertwining of demographic transition, the ecological and environmental crisis, and economic and social justice have produced a particular moment and a special set of circumstances for designers as well as communities in regional cities in Japan. This is the time when a shrinking portion of the population is asked to support an increasing group of people who will live longer, and when greater care must be taken in the utilization of natural resources, with seemingly insurmountable gaps between the rich and the poor. This moment and this milieu will also demand more of small regional cities, which need to use a shrinking tax base to provide a greater level of services for their communities. Ironically, this is also the moment when architecture and spatial revitalization can produce new and previously unimagined opportunities for the community and the larger territory.

3 See Kohei Saito, *Marx in the Anthropocene: Towards the Idea of Degrowth Communism* (Cambridge: Cambridge University Press, 2023). See also Kohei Saito, *Karl Marx's Ecosocialism: Capital, Nature, and the Unfinished Critique of Political Economy* (New York: Monthly Review Press, 2017).

1 Prospect

The Promise of an Architecture

Toyo Ito

Map depicting the locations of castle towns in Japan. There were at least 200 castle towns across the country, which were created during the Sengoku [Warring States] and Edo periods (15th–19th centuries). Their population sizes varied; some historians say that more than half of the Japanese cities with populations over 100,000 today originated as castle towns.

It's my belief that no places in Japan offer more potential for architecture, particularly public architecture, than the country's regional cities. This may sound like a surprising, even paradoxical, claim in light of social conditions in Japan today. Globalization has concentrated development investment in the great conurbations, while smaller cities in regions outside those metropolises suffer the consequences of this trend as they battle the effects of low birth rates and aging populations. Few people today believe that these outlying cities hold any kind of promise for architecture.

Surviving in the Shadow of Modernization

When we contemplate the future of Japan's regional cities, we can benefit from an understanding of their historical context. Soon after the Meiji Restoration, which began in 1868, the new government abolished the *han*, or feudal administrative units with a major castle at their center, and instituted a prefectural system in their stead. The nearly 300 *han* domains through which the shogunate had governed the country for over 250 years were replaced by 43 prefectures, variously known as *ken* or as *to* (Tokyo-to), *do* (Hokkai-do), or *fu* (Osaka-fu and Kyoto-fu), all under the rule of the central government. This reform retained the boundaries of the former *han* to some extent, even as the new prefectures were rezoned into units more conducive to nationally centralized administration. Consequently, the districts around the old castles (usually a particular city in each prefecture, but in some cases the entire prefecture) to this day retain something of the unique regional flavor they acquired during those centuries of *han* rule. In other words, most regional cities that boast a distinctive character were once castle towns.

These towns generally had a moat or moats encircling the castle, and the surrounding streets were laid out in mazelike patterns with numerous twists and turns for strategic purposes. (The regular grid of streets seen in Kyoto is a rare exception.) The strategy in question was not just a military one of impeding attacks on the castle. Japan sits in the Asian monsoon zone, and the seasonal rains have long provided inhabitants of the archipelago with many natural blessings. Nature has therefore traditionally been an object of veneration, awe, and affection to the Japanese, whose ways of thinking dramatically differ in this respect from those of the West, where nature is treated as an alien other, and architecture and cities as entities independent of nature. This difference in outlook was reflected in the design of castle towns as well; in Japan, they were laid out in patterns that accommodated the natural lay of the land, making ingenious use of the hills and rivers of the area. Even today we can see many instances of urban space that has inherited and preserved elements of the natural landscape, thanks to the influence on city planning of this

Kuwagata Keisai, *Edo hitomezu byobu* [Edo at a Glance], 1809. Courtesy of the Tsuyama City Museum. The six-panel screen shows a bird's-eye view of Edo (today's Tokyo) from above the east bank of the Sumida River looking west. The painter Kuwagata depicted more than 500 famous and historical sites, including the residences of feudal lords. The Edo castle is placed in the center, with Mt. Fuji at the back; however, the scenes of everyday life throughout are what make this screen unique.

Toyo Ito, Za-Koenji Public Theatre, Tokyo, 2008. A bird's-eye-view of Tokyo (Edo) created two hundred years after Kuwagata's. The public theater designed by Ito is the black solid mass in the left bottom of the photo.

traditional reverence for nature. It follows that such cities should be fertile ground for architecture that prioritizes a close relationship with nature.

Tokyo, too, was originally laid out around Edo Castle in a manner that utilized the natural terrain. But over the century and a half of modernization that followed the Meiji Restoration, the capital lost its harmonious spatial relationship with the land and water and transformed into the homogeneous urban space it is today.

Furthermore, the lord of a *han* castle was expected to be accomplished in not only the military but also the literary arts, and to be a patron of the same. The surrounding district would become a mecca for such artistic pursuits as the tea ceremony, flower arranging, and poetry, and many former castle towns still retain these activities. These cultural traditions were passed down in an inconspicuous manner in the shadow of modernization, neither undergoing major changes nor vanishing altogether. One might say that they have surreptitiously embedded themselves deep in the hearts of most Japanese. If we can bring the fondness for nature that still lurks in the Japanese heart to the surface, we should also be able to revitalize modern architecture, which has so thoroughly alienated itself from nature. That is why I have such high hopes for Japan's regional cities.

New Conditions for Architecture

Another reason I harbor great expectations for regional cities is that they already possess a social foundation as a community. Most such cities in Japan have populations ranging from several tens of thousands to several hundred thousand people. Cities of this size consist of groups of people who know each other or have at least met somewhere. When one builds a work of public architecture in such a city, people of all stripes—from kids on their way home from school to senior citizens living alone—are likely to frequent it. Facilities like libraries draw people of every age group, who meet there on a daily basis. Regional cities thus provide conditions that facilitate the pursuit of community activities.

One factor that contributes indirectly to the expanding opportunities for public architecture in these cities is the financial condition of regional municipalities these days. As a cost-cutting measure, many local governments now favor public facilities designed to handle multiple functions. These include not only cultural institutions like libraries, museums, and theaters, but also some city administrative functions, childcare facilities, and commercial establishments such as convenience stores. These new multifunctional public structures readily lend themselves to citizen participation, which in my view further enhances the possibilities for developing a new type of architecture.

By contrast, megacities like Tokyo and Osaka are growing increasingly uniform and their centers filling up with high-rise redevelopment projects dominated by offices, apartment complexes, luxury hotels, and commercial facilities. Here the priorities are convenience and profit, and community is not even a consideration.

This state of affairs can be attributed to the twin accessions of globalism and modernist architecture. Technological advances have made it possible to build modernist structures of the same design anywhere on the planet, and the globalist dream of turning the world into one vast "community" provides the incentive to do so. The inevitable result is the homogenization of the world's cities.

Redesigning Society through Architecture

Culture of the sort that is indispensable to the enrichment of urban life does not flourish in environments dominated by the massive redevelopment we now see spreading across Japan's largest urban centers. Nor can such culture survive in a given place if it is not rooted in the distinctive history and terrain of that place. Sadly, the cultural traditions that took root and thrived in various parts of premodern Japan are now being wiped out by the homogenization of its modernizing cities. At the same time, it is clear that the impasse that modernization has reached today is affecting Japanese society on a number of levels. The globalized economic system enriches only a few people engaged in the manipulation of information, while the economic disparities in society at large continue to widen; most people have lost any hope for a better life tomorrow. One senses that the time has come for cities to seek out new solutions.

One positive aspect of the modernization process to date that we must not overlook, however, is that Japan has already enjoyed a period of architectural innovation that produced many superb works of architecture in its regional cities. In the course of the nation's recovery from the Second World War, the first examples of a "new architecture" appeared in cities facing the Seto Inland Sea—Hiroshima, Kurashiki, Okayama, Imabari, Takamatsu. A generation of progressive mayors and prefectural governors in this region enlisted architects like Kenzo Tange to design inventive structures as they sought to build new communities atop the ashes of their firebombed cities. Most of these architects, moreover, skillfully incorporated elements of traditional Japanese aesthetics as well as people's aspirations for a new society into a modernist framework. We have much to learn from their initiative and energy.

Until now, we architects have tended to focus exclusively on Japan's metropolitan areas, notably Tokyo and Osaka. As I noted earlier, however, the globalism-influenced fixation of the big cities on economic wealth has caused their cultures to wither. Architecture has been reduced to a tool for economic pursuits and appears to have lost its capacity to reveal the future of society.

Kenzo Tange, Hiroshima Peace Memorial Museum, 1955. Hiroshima is one of the cities facing the Seto Inland Sea. The museum is composed of the main building (at left) and the east building with auxiliary facilities (at right).

If we seek a new architecture for the future, we should pay more attention to Japan's outlying cities. There are two particular aspects in which these cities offer tremendous opportunities for the architecture of tomorrow: their close relationship with the natural environment and their potential for community activities. Just as the postwar generation of architects was driven to produce pioneering works out of a desire to create a new society from the rubble of the cities, we need to aim high in our own aspirations to design a better society for tomorrow.

新規登録
インターネット
AV
予約
貸出・返却
自習席
受付
MAGAZINES

Toyo Ito, Minna no Mori / Gifu Media Cosmos, Gifu, 2015. Nicknamed "a forest for all," the Gifu Media Cosmos is a new type of public cultural complex. Here, the facility comprises the central library, a civic activity center, an auditorium, and a gallery.

onishimaki+hyakudayuki architects / o+h with Sanko Sekkei, Kioku / Kumamoto Earthquake Museum, Minami Aso Village, 2023. This museum, nicknamed "Kioku," holds the memories and lessons of the major earthquake that devastated the region in 2016.

2 Expanding the Architect's Role

Constructing a New Public

Kumiko Inui

Since Japan began to motorize in the 1960s, cities outside the major urban hubs have undergone a hollowing-out of the downtowns where their civic functions were once concentrated. The relentless development of shopping malls, megastores, and suburban housing complexes has dispersed these functions outward.

Regional cities have attempted to revitalize their cores through the implementation of various urban redevelopment policies, but the concurrent easing of restrictions on megastore development has impeded these efforts, instead accelerating the outward sprawl of these cities. With giant "category-killer" stores lining the roads and offering easy access to all manner of merchandise, local residents have come to associate them with the good life and increasingly forgo trips downtown. This mentality in turn makes it difficult for citizens to challenge the massive amounts of tax money expended on road construction and expansion, which further exacerbates these changes in the city.

Until Japan began experiencing a salient downturn in population, it was possible to argue that suburban sprawl and downtown revitalization were not mutually exclusive. Only when population loss became an issue did people begin to treat the questions of how to make cities more compact, reinvigorate their cores, and expand public transit networks as part of the same problem. Postwar urban planning in Japan had sought to balance the optimization of land use with revitalization of the economy through deregulation, leaving it to later generations to resolve the inherent contradictions between these two policies.

The contradictions generated by policies predicated on motorization may be said, for example, to lie behind the recent tragic increase in auto accidents caused by elderly drivers. As Japan's population ages, cracks are beginning to appear in the "my-car" lifestyle.

Sprawling while Hollowing

This diffusion of cities is not just a Japanese phenomenon. Books like *Cities without Cities: An Interpretation of the Zwischenstadt* (Routledge, 2003) by Thomas Sieverts show how rural areas are urbanizing in Europe as well. Sieverts explains that cities are decentralizing while "in-between" areas that are neither urban nor rural proliferate. It appears that globalization not only consolidates the production and distribution of goods and services, but also destroys family-run manufacturing and commerce, thereby contributing to the decay of the city centers where these businesses were concentrated, in what has become a standard pattern of urban change.

Today, when this urban diffusion is a global trend, local governments must decide what to do about the decentralization of their cities. After Japan's population peaked in 2008 and embarked on its current conspicuous decline, urban planners began to shift their approach to institutional design in the

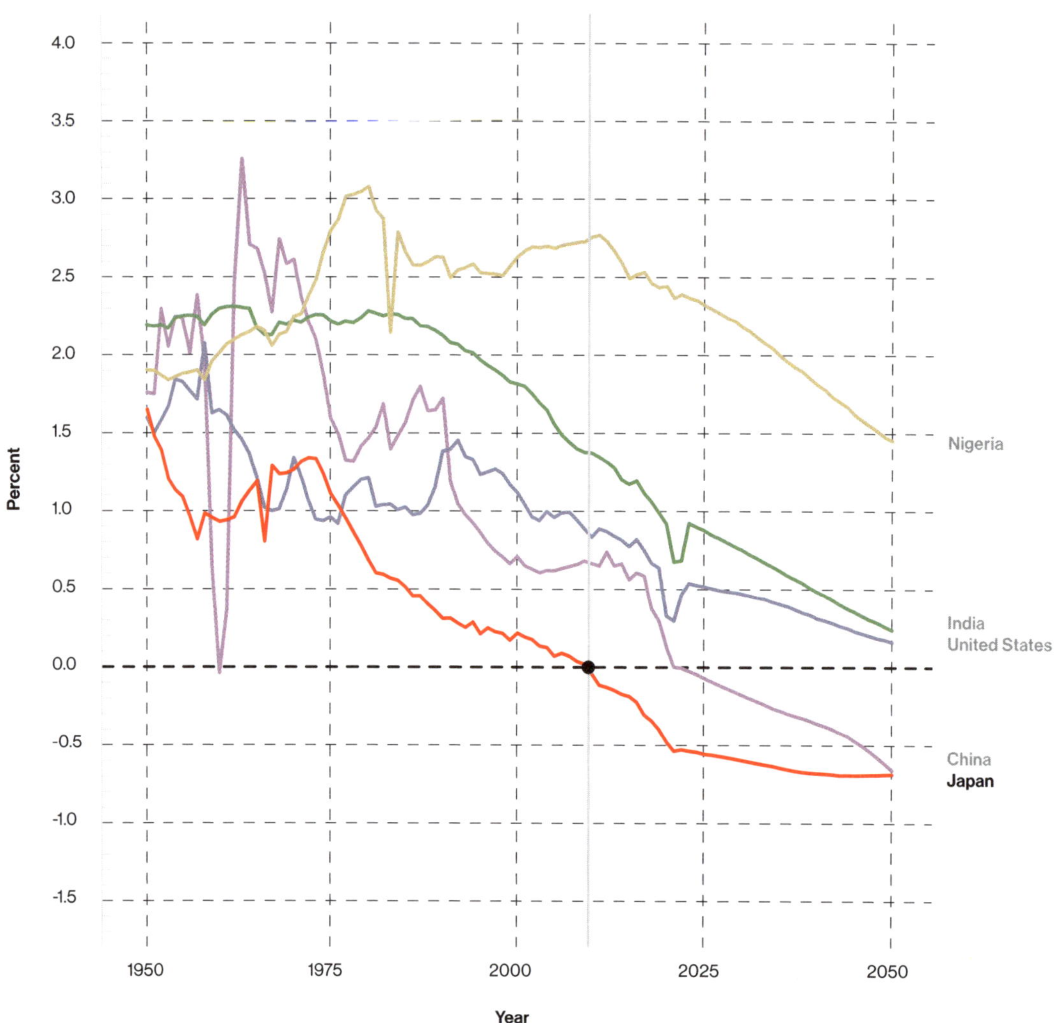

A country-by-country comparison of population growth rates projected over the next 30 years.
Source © 2022 United Nations, DESA, World Population Prospects 2022.

direction of making cities more compact by prioritizing the optimization of land use. In this context, a city center with adequate public transit and other infrastructure was repositioned as key to the compaction process. A system for refining municipal master planning, known as "location normalization plans," was formulated to promote the long-term compaction of cities through investment spurred by tax breaks, but these plans did not aim to preserve downtowns in their current state or restore them to a previous state.

Most city centers in Japan were rebuilt from the ashes left by the firebombings of World War II. With their haphazard mix of buildings hastily constructed during the postwar economic boom and the oddly ornate structures of the subsequent bubble years, these downtowns can hardly be described as attractive. They are a far cry from the European urban centers where visible vestiges of the old city survive and the townscape is valued as a tourism resource. Moreover, they are dotted with open-air parking lots where shops once stood and thus lack the sense of density that makes a downtown feel like a downtown. Having lost the economic and social elements that once sustained their vitality, such districts are not likely to draw investors through tax breaks alone. Institutional policies cannot do the job on their own; efforts to improve the appeal of a city center must take place on multiple fronts.

The Architect's Role Reevaluated

In recent years, these circumstances have drawn many architects to engage with efforts to revive Japan's regional downtowns. Initially they were often asked to design outlandish buildings that would ostensibly serve as catalysts for revitalization. Nowadays, however, a different kind of impact is sought.

If these regional city centers are to be resuscitated, it is essential that we devise creative methods of reusing the hollowed-out "shells" of these downtowns, however negligible their value may appear to be today. Architects must engage in scrupulous local research, identify existing physical, economic, and social assets that can serve as resources, work closely with local citizens to unearth the forgotten or ignored value and potential of these assets, and apply this knowledge to the development of new, site-specific ideas for revitalization. These ideas can then be realized in the form of architecture and the programs that take place in it. Lately, local governments have begun to recognize what architects have to offer in this area, and have come to rely on their contributions to civic revitalization efforts.

The city of Nobeoka, Miyazaki Prefecture, where I have engaged in just such a revitalization project, was typical in the state of decay of its downtown. Nearly all the businesses lining the main shopping street had been shuttered and were surrounded by a growing expanse of open-air parking lots. The entire town seemed threadbare and empty. And yet—perhaps thanks to

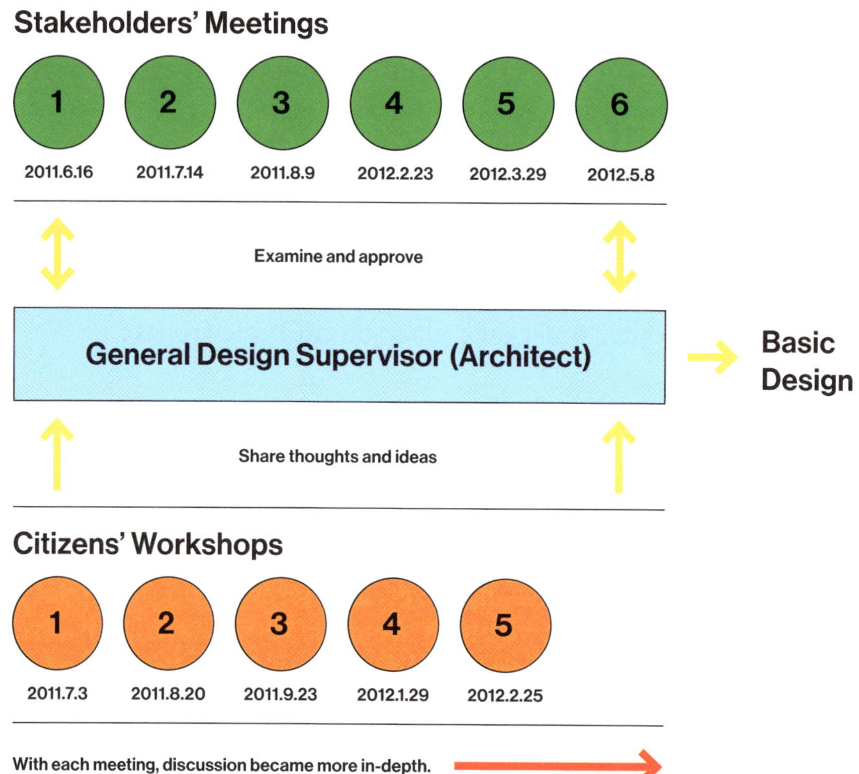

Diagram illustrating the basic planning phase of the Nobeoka project. Prior to designing the complex, all the stakeholders—multiple transportation companies, the associations of merchants and business operators in the neighborhood and the city, knowledgeable professionals in relevant fields, and the general design supervisor (i.e., the commissioned architect)—held meetings to discuss the overall vision and strategy for the complex as well as tangible matters related to the design. The plans and opinions generated in these stakeholder meetings were then shared with local volunteers over the course of discussion workshops, whereby volunteers met with the architect to share their thoughts and ideas for the building's use, as well as other intangible matters related to the design. Diagram courtesy of studio-L.

the subtropical air and sunlight for which Miyazaki is known—the mood of the town was not particularly depressed. The bars and restaurants appeared to thrive at night, and life in the neighborhoods outside the city center seemed pleasant. In other words, the citizens of Nobeoka enjoyed a reasonably fulfilling lifestyle; it was only the downtown district that was in trouble. The problems it faced were primarily structural in nature, such as the prevalence of absentee ownership of downtown real estate. However, it seemed feasible that an architectural project might alter impressions of the city center and enrich the lifestyle options of the people of Nobeoka. I took on this project with that goal in mind.

An Organic Relationship between Space and Users' Activities

The objective of the Nobeoka Station Area Development Project was to revitalize Nobeoka's city center by redeveloping the area in front of the train station. This required a community development program that extended beyond the purview of architectural design. It was my first experience with full-scale community development, so I began by seeking advice and guidance from Ryo Yamazaki, a community designer heading studio-L, who was already working with the city of Nobeoka. He advised the city that it needed a place for citizens' activities, not a commercial facility or one with specific functions. Furthermore, he conducted multiple workshops in which local citizens discussed what sorts of activities should be supported. We developed our actual program from the views expressed in Mr. Yamazaki's workshops.

When the work process includes meeting users face-to-face and ascertaining their specific wishes, even a public architecture project acquires the intimate feel of a house design project. Unlike conventional public architecture projects that produce anonymous multipurpose spaces for large numbers of unidentified users, this one demanded that we create an organic, interactive relationship between the architectural space and its users' activities by providing facilities that would stimulate the activities taking place there and highlight their appeal. Only in a regional city where users can be clearly identified is it possible to shape a work of architecture through grass-roots citizen participation. In these workshops many people also declared their interest in activities that would serve to revitalize their town, not merely to entertain themselves. This active stance of engaging with one's city as something that is part of oneself exemplifies the vision of a "new publicness" built on public-private partnership, an approach that began to gain cachet in the wake of the Great East Japan Earthquake of 2011. The progressiveness of their point of view opened my eyes to the possibilities to be found in regional cities.

Also novel to me was the expansion of the architect's role: we found ourselves involved in the project from the program-making stage, before starting on the actual design. Ordinarily one thinks of architectural design as a process of giving concrete form to a plan that has already been devised. This time, however, it seemed that the design process, based as it is on a knowledge of space and place, was being utilized to facilitate decisions at the planning stage on what to do, where, and how—or even on the fundamental question of what sorts of people and activities this place would need to accommodate. With both the planning and designing phases now falling under the purview of "design," a circuit was formed whereby we would revisit decisions at the planning level while in the midst of the designing phase. This circuit fostered the development of a more organic relationship between program and program, program and form, and so on.

Concurrently with the program-developing stage, we were also asked to submit proposals on the layout, external appearance, and other elements of the project associated with the landscape design aspect of civic revitalization. Here, too, it was a new experience to have the design phase overlap with this process instead of coming later. In specific terms this entailed incorporating decisions on the appropriate scale of the project into the landscape design process, as a result of which we were able to come up with a scale that was a good fit for the city. If we had followed the conventional procedure of first defining the programs as a table of areas, then giving them form, the resulting facility would surely have been overscaled.

Creating Relationality through Architecture

At the actual design stage, we struggled to achieve a balance between affording a degree of freedom to the activities of users and operators of the facility, and creating an environment that would encourage activities. This was not a project intended only for activities with specific objectives, like a community center. It was imperative that the design foster an atmosphere conducive to casual use for no particular reason—a place where people would feel free to hang out. To that end we decided to design a frame-type structure forming an irregular grid. Through the placement of skylights and atriums here and there throughout the structure, we sought to create a variety of comfortable spaces that would feel welcoming to diverse civic activities.

We also prioritized the facility's connection to the landscape and functions surrounding it. The flat, open structure of Nobeoka Station exuded a sense of continuity and unity with the adjacent townscape not seen in urban train stations. Moreover, most of the buildings and residences around the station were built in the sixties or earlier, a time when construction had yet to be entirely industrialized. Though designed in the modern era, they retained handcrafted elements. The station house itself was a ferroconcrete structure typical of the seventies in its unadorned simplicity. To harmonize with these appealing aspects of the station and its environs, we used extremely ordinary materials—concrete, steel, glass—like those of the station house, and also emulated its appearance in the height of our structure and the thickness and span of its columns. Our aim was to maintain that feeling of continuity, as if the new building were an extension of the old one. We also opened up numerous apertures to frame views typical of a station; created sightlines that guided the eyes through various openings beyond the confines of the station yard and the project; and sought to optimize functional connections with nearby facilities, for example by placing the toilets near the adjoining police box as a crime-prevention measure. Thus we employed a variety of means to establish close links between the station, the town, and our project.

Our work on the project extended to supervising the redesign of the rotary in front of the station and the repair of the existing station house, thus giving me the opportunity to take on some civil engineering-related tasks. Additionally, the determination of a project size appropriate to the scale of Nobeoka's downtown district and of the city's economy was intertwined with the process of securing funding sources for the project. In this instance, we were able to participate in discussions of fundamentals that would normally have been held behind closed doors by city administrators. I am pretty certain that the conditions that allowed us to undertake tasks ranging from design to supervision, and even to join discussions of budgetary issues, were a product of the relative discretion that public officials in regional cities enjoy. I was personally able to engage with local administrators regarding every process involved in the project; I also feel that we succeeded in prioritizing the place-making, space-making implications of every decision we reached. Consequently, we were able to proceed with close interplay among the aspects of civic revitalization, civil engineering and design, project planning, and administrative programming. The result was the creation of an area in which station and city form an integrated entity that transcends the bounds of the actual site.

This project could not have succeeded without the presence in Nobeoka of a substantial number of highly aware citizens and administrators. I have no doubt that there are many other relatively small regional cities that nurture this same attitude—the imagination to take a personal stake in the future of one's city, and the drive to put one's thoughts into action. This is a sensibility and a power that can be nurtured precisely because the users and designers of architecture are closer together in such communities. And what could be more effective than architecture-based revitalization as a means of growing and consolidating this power into a solid base for community activities? I believe that this very process can serve as a new mode of development, one that is needed to make a city a truly fulfilling place to live.

References:
Shin Aiba, *History of Urban Planning in the Heisei Era*. Tokyo: Kadensha, 2021.
Thomas Sieverts, *Cities without Cities: An Interpretation of the Zwischenstadt*. Routledge, 2003.

Nobeoka Station Area Development Project

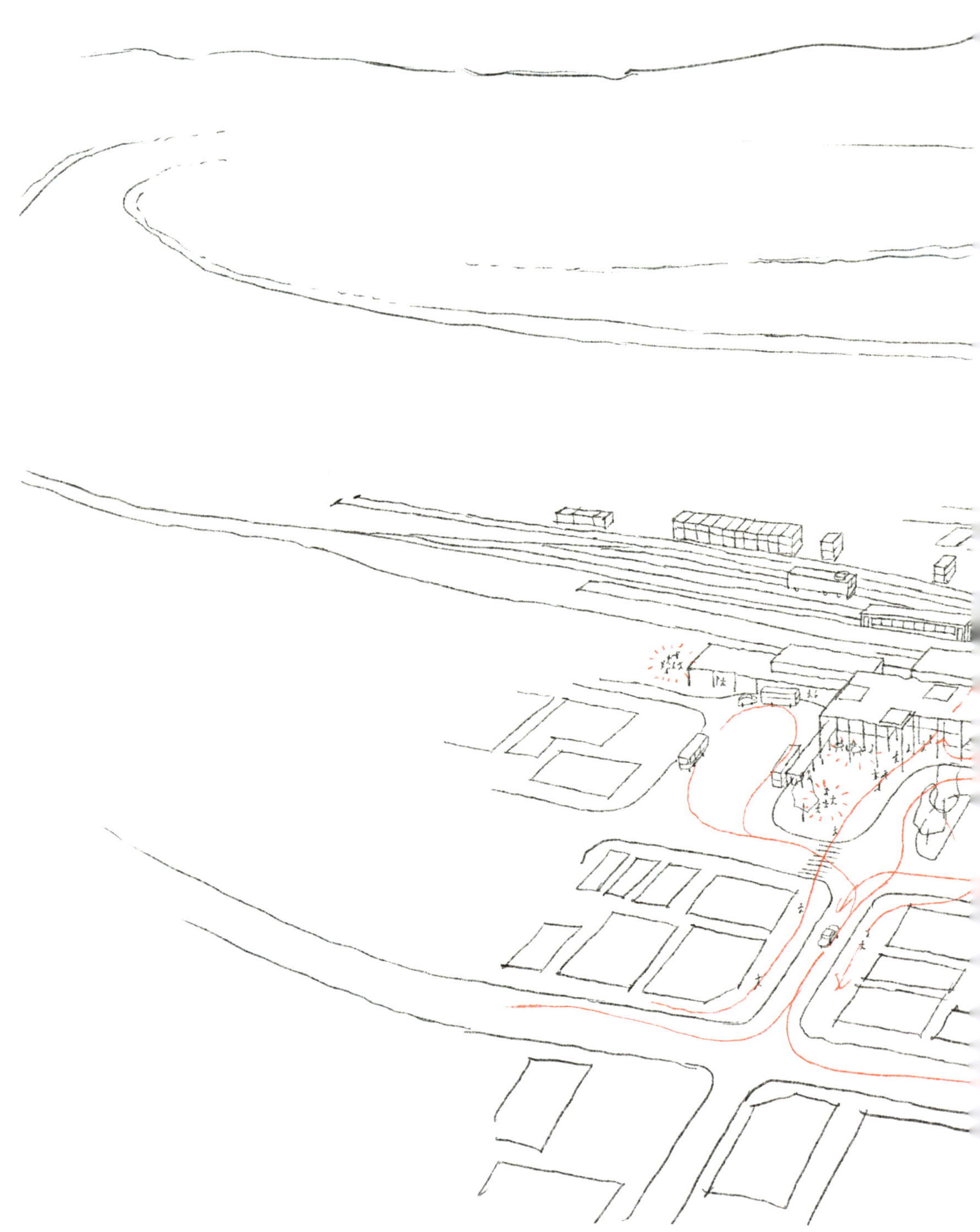

A sketch by Inui of the various flow lines of user traffic to be generated by this redevelopment project.

DESIGN: INUI ARCHITECTS
LOCATION: NOBEOKA CITY, MIYAZAKI PREFECTURE
COMPLETION: 2018

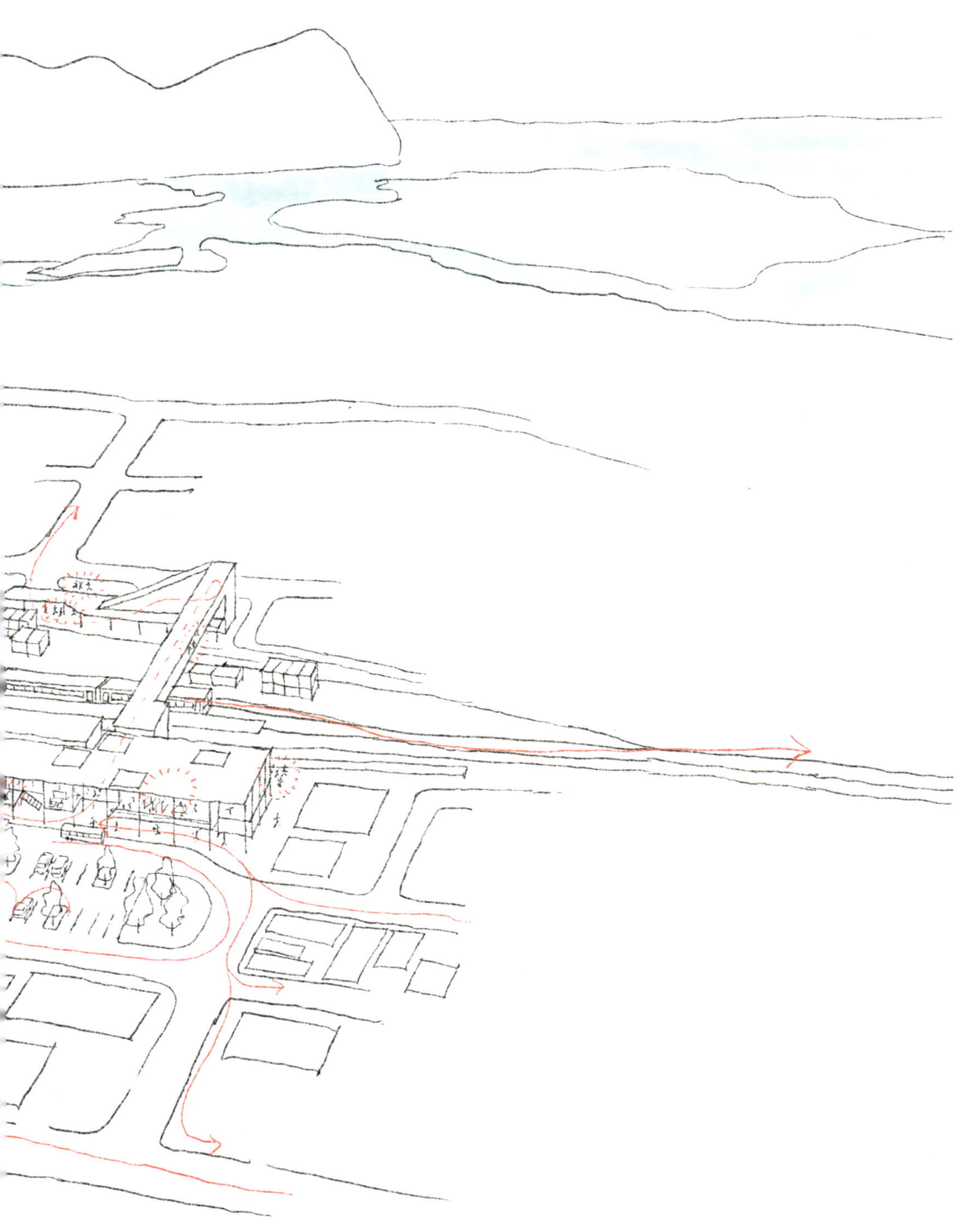

延
NOBE

The central train terminal of a regional city in Japan is typically marked by a towering high-rise. Instead of stacking floors atop the old station building in Nobeoka, the architect added a new, low-rise multipurpose building in front of the terminal to provide local residents with a variety of reasons to gather there.

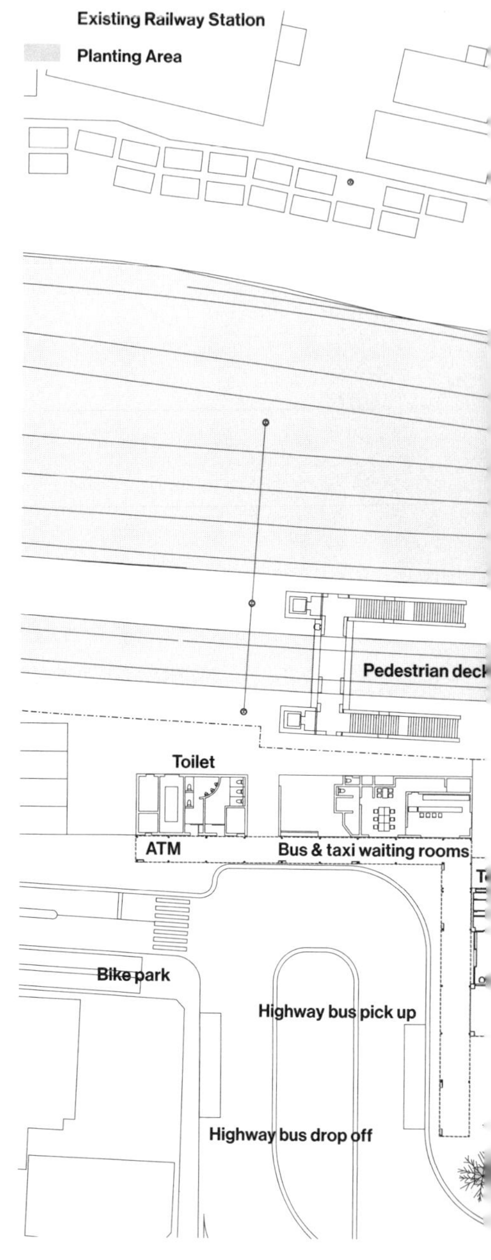

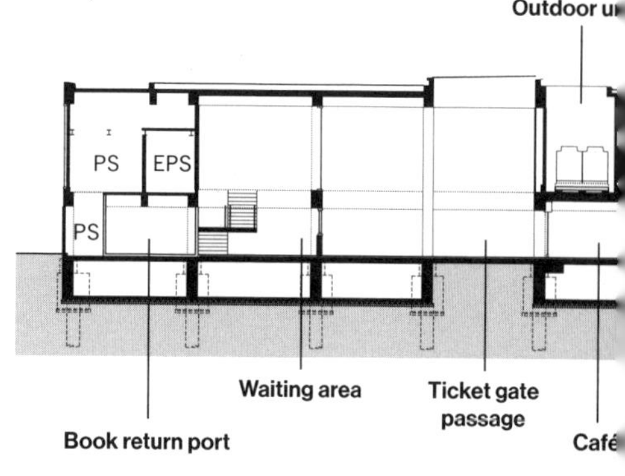

Top: In the multipurpose building created between the station and the traffic circle, people cross paths as they board trains, attend public programs, and visit the café or library. Bottom: Spaces for different programs rhythmically alternate from unit to unit inside the irregular grid structure.

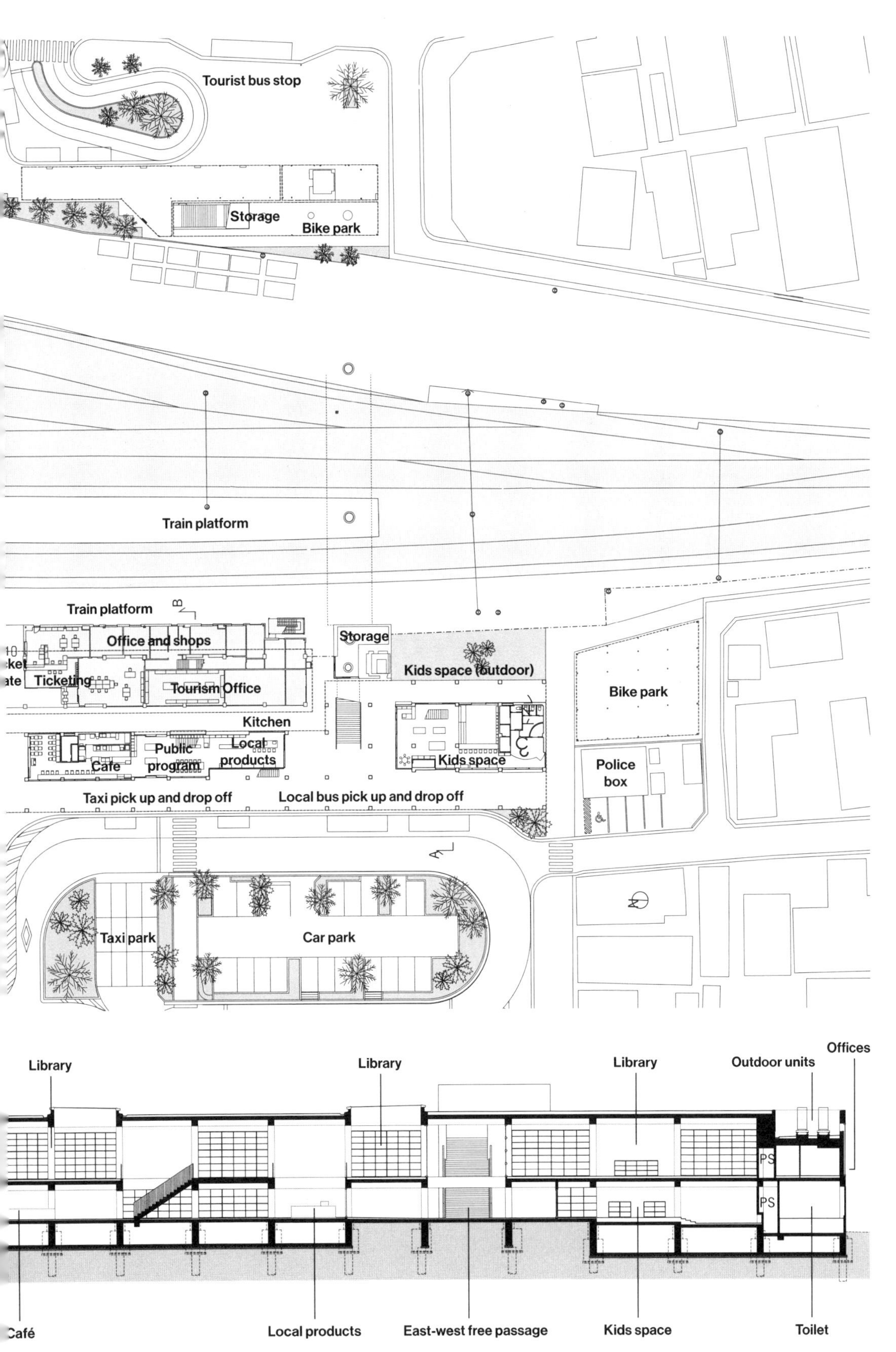

Tourist bus stop
Storage
Bike park
Train platform
Train platform
Office and shops
Ticketing
Tourism Office
Storage
Kids space (outdoor)
Bike park
Kitchen
Public program
Local products
Cafe
Kids space
Police box
Taxi pick up and drop off
Local bus pick up and drop off
Taxi park
Car park
Library
Library
Library
Outdoor units
Offices
PS
PS
Café
Local products
East-west free passage
Kids space
Toilet

Inui says that her research on the spontaneous and anonymous generation of "little spaces" taught her that "a simple frame and a diversity of slabs and apertures deriving from it" can produce appealing spaces of this sort.

The side of the building facing the station rotary is a semi-outdoor space that forms a natural transition between interior and exterior. The design is an outgrowth of Inui's research on "little spaces."

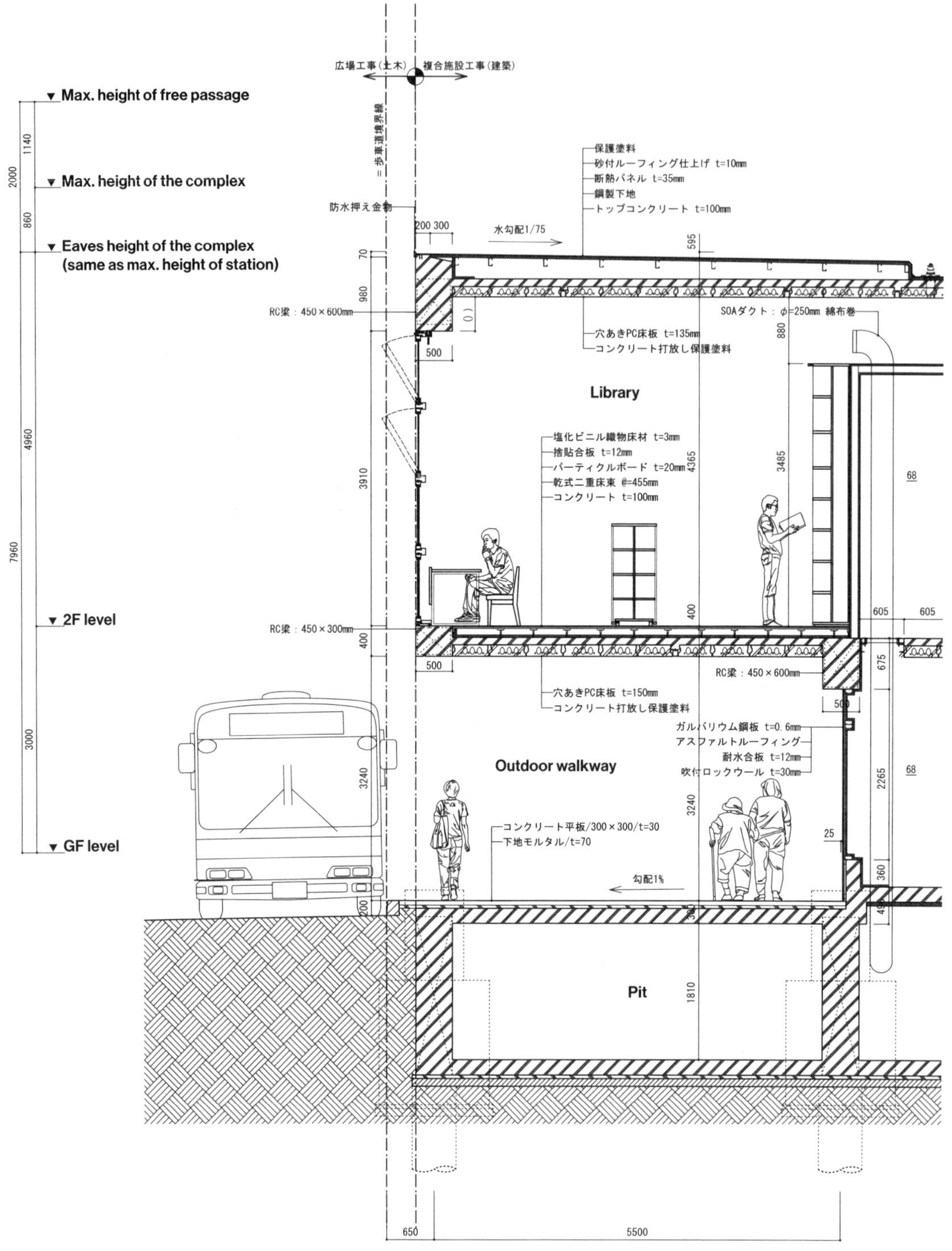

The second floor is situated at a lower height than is typical in such buildings. Bringing the second floor closer to the street and the station concourse visually links activities on that floor with the movements of people at ground level.

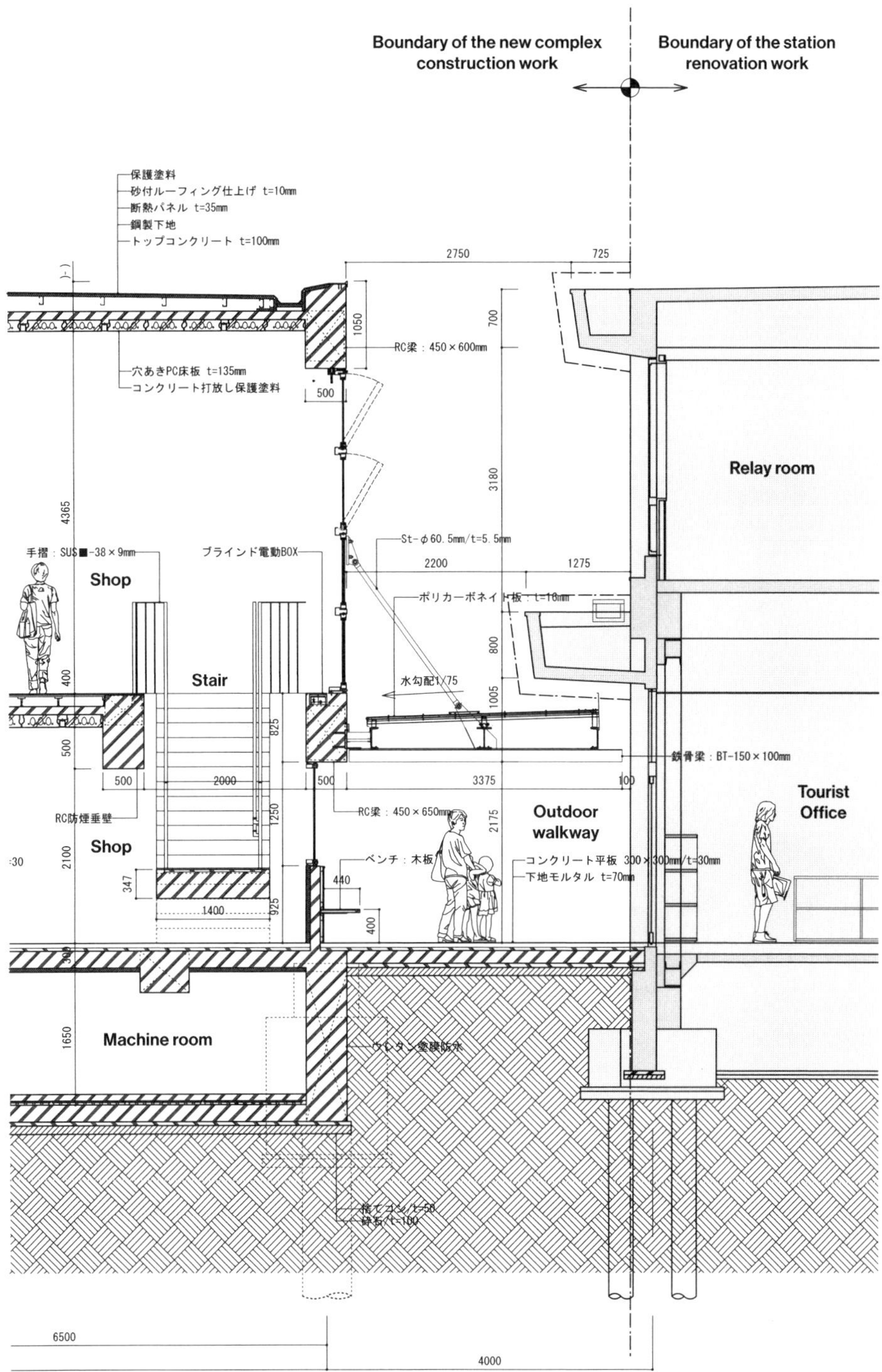

Setting the second floor only three meters above the ground also helps encourage people to use the stairs. People can climb them with ease, and there is no need for a landing.

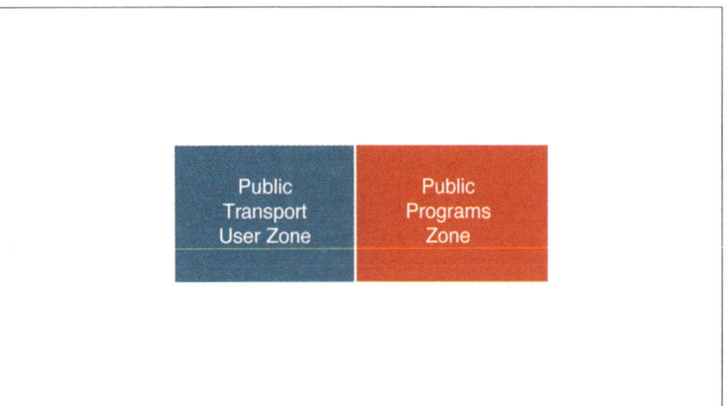

1. Public programs are placed next to the station

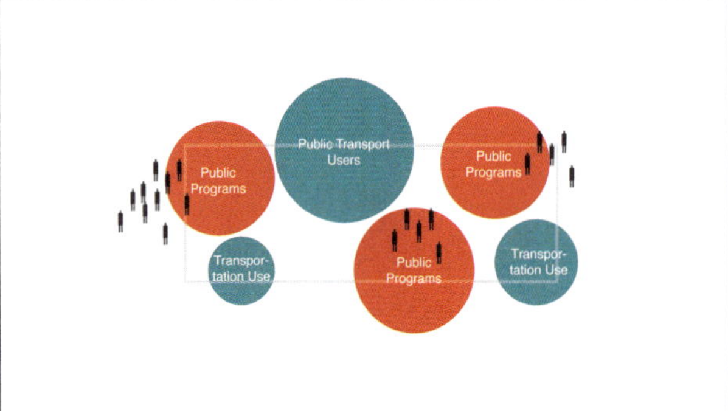

2. Public transport users and public program participants are put together

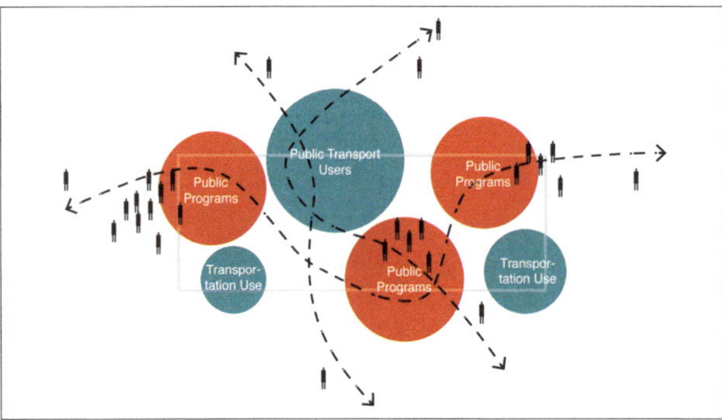

3. Visitors to the city activate the place

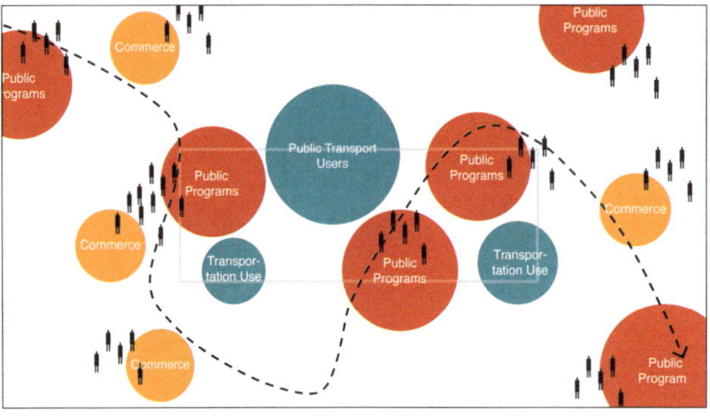

4. Positive spiral of urban reactivation

Mixed-rice model of combining a station and public programs: Inui's approach to revitalizing a city in decline is what she calls the *mazegohan*, or "mixed rice," model of scattering a number of stimulating projects throughout the project area.

"We opened up numerous apertures to frame views typical of a station and created sightlines that guide the eyes through various openings beyond the confines of the station yard and the project" [Inui].

An aggregation of welcoming spaces invites the people who gather here to engage in diverse activities. By dividing the building into numerous "little spaces" for varying functions, the plan increases the areas of contact between these activities. The effect is of a relaxed, festive gathering place where people's sightlines and flow lines freely intersect.

Scattered throughout this building are layout strategies that create visible yet loosely defined connections among the diverse user activities and between interior and exterior.

Miyajimaguchi Passenger Terminal

DESIGN: INUI ARCHITECTS
LOCATION: HATSUKAICHI CITY, HIROSHIMA PREFECTURE
COMPLETION: 2020

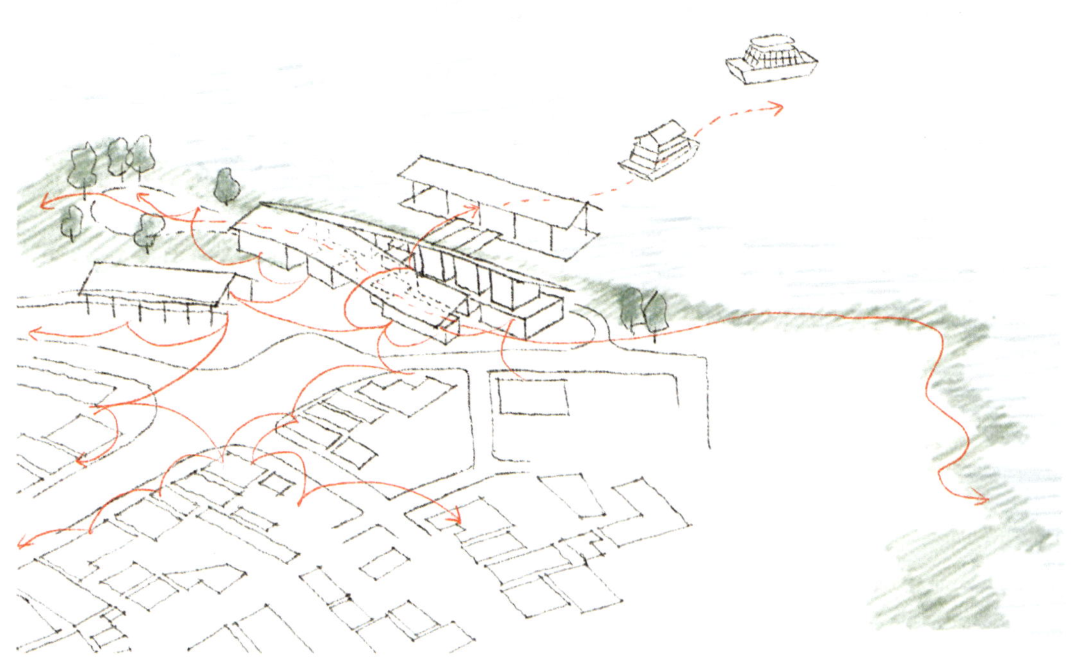

Revitalizing a town via its transportation infrastructure. A sketch by Inui.

Top: The view from a ferry arriving from Miyajima shows how faithfully the color and texture of the pier and terminal roofs have been fine-tuned to match that of the sea. Bottom: This transportation facility seems designed to provide a bright, airy interface with the World Heritage Site island of Miyajima by incorporating the pleasant ambience of the seashore.

ななうら丸
禁煙
危ないので柵より先に
出ないでください。

The roof of the pier that stretches alongside the sea is another product of Inui's research on anonymous architecture. As Inui wrote in her book *Little Spaces*, "The view the roof frames of the sea and the lush green mountains is simple and bold, its vibrancy enhanced by the clean lines of the structure's design. Here, the scenery is the star."

Choosing Quality of Life over the Bottom Line

Jun Aoki

Japan has three major metropolitan areas. Greater Tokyo consists of the prefectures of Tokyo, Kanagawa, Saitama, and Chiba; Greater Osaka, of Osaka, Hyogo, Kyoto, and Nara; and Greater Nagoya, of Aichi, Gifu, and Mie. Together these three regions take up about 14 percent of Japan's land area and are home to 50 percent of its population—a conspicuous degree of concentration. Of particular note is Greater Tokyo, which occupies no more than 3.5 percent of Japan's total area yet contains nearly 30 percent of its population. Also, while the proportion of the country's population that lives in the Osaka and Nagoya conurbations remains fairly constant, that of Greater Tokyo increases from year to year. While the tendency for people to migrate to cities is a nationwide trend, it is particularly extreme in Tokyo. Conversely, most of the rest of Japan is emptying out at a feverish pace.

The primary reason for this population concentration in Greater Tokyo is the economic wealth of the region, which boasts an average income as much as 30 percent higher than elsewhere. With young people all over Japan leaving home for Tokyo, the elderly are increasingly concentrated in outlying regions, which then suffer from declining birth rates, causing regional economies to shrink in a vicious cycle. This is a structural problem for Japanese society, with no solution in sight.

From Boosting the Economy to Boosting the Quality of Life

My studio has carried out a considerable number of projects in regions outside the major urban areas. In all of these undertakings, one of our primary objectives has been to improve the quality of everyday life for people in that area.

One of our earliest projects was the Mamihara Bridge (1995), a small span across a river in a depopulated mountainous area on the border between Kumamoto and Miyazaki Prefectures on the southern island of Kyushu. The local government requested that we design the bridge as a kind of icon or *objet d'art* that would draw tourists to the area. However, tourists might visit the area for that purpose once, at most. There might be an initial surge of visitors right after the bridge was completed, but that would gradually subside. What was really needed was a space that local residents would be happy to have in their community. Like other depopulated areas, this one was losing its young people to the cities. I thought that we should design a bridge that these young people would come to identify with their hometown when they saw it on their trips home.

So if the bridge was not to be a tourist attraction, what, then, was it? I thought of it as a road: not a destination in itself, but a space linking destinations. A bridge is a section of a much longer entity—a road—that changes form as it passes over a river. Nowadays roads are diminished presences defined solely by their function as conduits for traffic. But once upon a time, they were places where people met and interacted with one another, where peddlers and

Tourists gathered on Mamihara Bridge watch palanquin bearers splash water on a statue of the bodhisattva Jizo as they carry it through the river as part of a fire-prevention prayer festival.

street performers set up shop, where children played. Due to their role as places of transit, roads served as multipurpose spaces that supported many functions at once. I wanted to transform the road above this river into that sort of space.

At the riverbank, the road divides into the upper and lower bridge decks. The two tiers diverge, reach their greatest distance apart in the middle of the river, and then grow closer again until they become one on the other side. The upper deck is open to motor vehicles, but the lower one is for pedestrians only. That slight modification transforms the lower deck into a space like an arched bridge turned upside-down. Where the lower deck slopes gently downward and then back up again, the upper deck serves as a canopy to protect it from the rain; where it is closest to the river, it is bathed in a gentle breeze. This pleasant space is the result of no special design, just a slight detail applied to a conventional road.

Since the bridge was completed, the lower deck has become a nightly gathering place where people sit on straw mats in a circle, drinking and chatting; it also serves as audience seating for events held on the river and as a sanctuary where one can sit quietly reading a book. In the outlying districts of Japan, architecture is often designed as a means of gaining some direct economic benefit. However, there are practical limits to such conceptions. My design for the Mamihara Bridge grew out of my conviction that it is more important to create architecture that enriches the quality of life of the community by utilizing the unique potential of that particular environment.

Architecture in Close Proximity to Its Users

More often than not, this approach leads to confrontation with local politicians and administrators. Take, for example, a common building type: the civic hall. This is a facility centered around an auditorium with a typical capacity of around 1,000 and built for the purpose of holding coming-of-age ceremonies, lectures, concerts, plays, and other presentations or performances by and for the community. City administrators occasionally see such projects as a vehicle for enhancing their own prestige. They may want a facility whose splendor rivals or even exceeds that of the halls they have seen in the big cities. The fact is, however, that famous orchestras and the like simply do not perform in small outlying cities. Out-of-town acts consist mostly of Japanese popular singers and other entertainers. Nonetheless, the local movers and shakers will want a space that could be mistaken for one of the great concert halls of Europe, and if they get their way, the town will be saddled with astronomical maintenance costs that it will be hard put to cover.

When I was asked to design a civic hall in Miyoshi, a small city surrounded by mountains in Hiroshima Prefecture, I envisioned a place where residents could perform the locally celebrated Kagura, an ancient ceremonial

The architect opened his "branch office" near the project site early in the project process to enhance communication with the future users and local collaborators. Top: a shuttered downtown bakery was adapted as the first construction-site office, which also served to host different kinds of local gatherings. Bottom: local people also used the first floor of the on-site office for the project's pilot programs.

Shinto dance. However, that idea was summarily dismissed as irrelevant by the municipal authorities. Even so, we adhered to our original concept by designing a hall whose form and functionality minimized the distinction between performers and audience so that citizens could easily participate in both roles. The upshot was that the opening event featured seven local Kagura troupes who performed there from morning to night.

While all public architecture is ostensibly built for the purpose of serving the citizenry, the distance between such facilities and the people they serve is closer in smaller regional communities than in the big cities. Projects like this one remind me that the true client in such cases is not the politicians or the bureaucrats, but the citizens themselves.

An Endlessly Evolving Organism

That said, it is no easy thing to deal directly with local residents. If you want to hear their opinions and hold workshops for that purpose, those who show up will be the ones with the loudest voices and the most vociferous demands. It is hard to ascertain the views of the "silent majority" who do not, or cannot, raise their own voices. And yet they are indeed the majority. Moreover, residents never take the initiative to participate in such meetings, and this is true for the big-mouthed and the silent alike. Most citizens are passive, believing that the government will take care of things for them.

When I designed Bunjiro and Jujiro, two municipal facilities for Tokamachi, a small city in a mountainous area of Niigata Prefecture, I made an effort to hear the views of "small-voiced" citizens and to find and nurture among them people who would be proactive participants in the design process.

The project entailed the renovation of two buildings in the depressed central district of the city. Tokamachi's decline had begun in the 1980s. For over thirty years, the local government and citizenry had launched various projects aimed at economic revitalization, but after repeated failures the city had given up on such efforts. The two buildings in question had been purchased by the city when local businesses could no longer afford to maintain them. There were no plans in place for their redesign; the city's sole stipulation was that they contribute to the revitalization of the community, not of the economy per se.

We began by having two of our younger staffers relocate to Tokamachi, where we rented a shuttered downtown bakery and opened a "branch office" there to serve as our on-site workplace. With only two staff on hand, however, most of the space remained empty. The all-glass storefront faced a street and made it easy for passersby to look inside. I asked the staffers to get to know and talk to as many people as they could. My thinking was that we might identify the unspoken wishes of the townspeople by listening to them, not by holding workshops.

Since the bakery layout was inconvenient as it stood, we made some simple renovations with the help of local people we met who worked in the construction business. When we built a model of our project, it attracted people's interest, and passersby would come in and chat. Now that we had a space in town where a certain number of people could congregate, it became a hangout for the construction people who had helped with the refurbishing. Since the city offices were closed at night, it also served as a place where we could meet with residents. A group that assisted shut-in children asked to rent our space for an event. When a cherished tea house was threatened with demolition by a redevelopment project, concerned citizens came to us, asking for advice on what could be done about it. People showed up nightly to eat or chat with one another. Before we knew it, our studio's "branch office" had become a "branch office" for a variety of groups.

Over time, our discussions of the design and programming aspects of our renovation project with the people who gathered at our office evolved into two groups: the "tangibles" team, which addressed the design, and the "intangibles" team, which worked on the programming. When the plans were ready and we began work on the sites, we vacated the bakery and reopened our "branch office" to the public on the first floor of the temporary structure built to serve as the construction site office. A local resident set up a café there on weekends, and someone else opened a dance studio. Yet another volunteer scheduled a series of lectures for high-school students. We began teaching a do-it-yourself carpentry class so that local residents could do simple work on the facilities once they were finished.

We moved the tea house that had been slated for demolition into one of the new facilities. This is a region that gets several meters of snowfall in the winter, so we shifted the outer walls of the buildings inward to the first row of interior columns and created narrow roofed open spaces facing the street. These spaces became venues for events ranging from markets to fashion shows. Fixtures facing the street were placed at a height of only 1,800 mm to encourage citizens to adapt each space as they liked. Finally, the "branch office" that had begun in a bakery and then moved to the construction site became the management office for the two renovated spaces.

This approach to design meant that the project did not end with the completion of renovations and the transfer of the facilities to the city. We continue to serve as consultants on updates to the project. Every year we are invited to a briefing session on what is known as Bunjiro and Jujiro's "birthday." This may have been a renovation design project, but the architecture is not a finished product. Rather, it is a living entity designed to enhance the everyday life of the community through perpetual interaction with an ever-changing environment.

One memorable consequence of this endeavor was the harsh criticism of our efforts by the director of an art festival that is held in this area every three years. The director argued that his team had proposed the festival as part of a "shot in the arm" strategy to resuscitate the region because it lacked the strength to revitalize itself, and that's what they have been doing for many years. What we did, he claimed, was the precise opposite. However, my belief is that instead of giving someone on their deathbed a life-prolonging "shot in the arm," architects must do what they can to enable such cities to revive themselves.

The Potential of Regional Architecture Today

Throughout Japan these days, in big cities and outlying areas alike, priority is given to development projects that pay economic dividends. It goes without saying that the economic aspect is crucial where the continuity of a project is concerned. But in places where economic revitalization is structurally prohibitive, the pursuit of immediate, short-term benefits is likely to accelerate the impoverishment of the region, just as slash-and-burn agriculture inhibits the recuperative power of the soil and accelerates its desertification.

What is needed, in short, is to enrich the soil itself, and that is what architects must attempt to do. Even if they are asked to come up with icons, objects, and so on, they should instead expand the concept of architecture and consider how the entire architectural process, from conception to planning to implementation, can be placed in the service of cultivating new sources of enrichment and values for community life. Such practices, I am convinced, will directly or indirectly impart restorative power to the community and enable the people in it to create a future for themselves by harnessing their own initiative.

Mamihara Bridge

The structure is that of a steel-frame Vierendeel truss modified in the shape of a pair of lips. The upper and lower chords and the support columns are all structural elements.

DESIGN: AS
LOCATION: YAMATOCHO TOWN, KUMAMOTO PREFECTURE
COMPLETION: 1995

Mamihara Bridge is located at the end of the main street of an old inn town that flourished as a transportation hub in Kyushu.

The upper deck of the bridge is open to both motor and foot traffic, while the lower deck is for pedestrians only. Made of *sugi* cedar, the floor of the lower deck contains two large circular apertures. In summer this promenade is in shadow and benefits from the breezes flowing over the cool water below.

Tokamachi Activity Center Jujiro
Tokamachi Communication Center Bunjiro

DESIGN: AS
LOCATION: TOKAMACHI CITY, NIIGATA PREFECTURE
COMPLETION: 2016

The revitalization project for Tokamachi entailed an unusual design process. Before starting work on the design, the architects relocated to the city and made the acquaintance of local residents, listened to their views, and worked with them to develop programs for the architecture.

本町 三丁目通り

Two facilities on Tokamachi's main shopping street were designed to serve as "pressure points" to stimulate the district's revitalization. The building at far right is Jujiro, an activity center for local residents. The second building from the left is Bunjiro, a "communication center" for the community. Occupying old office buildings, both facilities contain a variety of rooms suitable for events ranging from workshops and creative activities to reading circles and lectures.

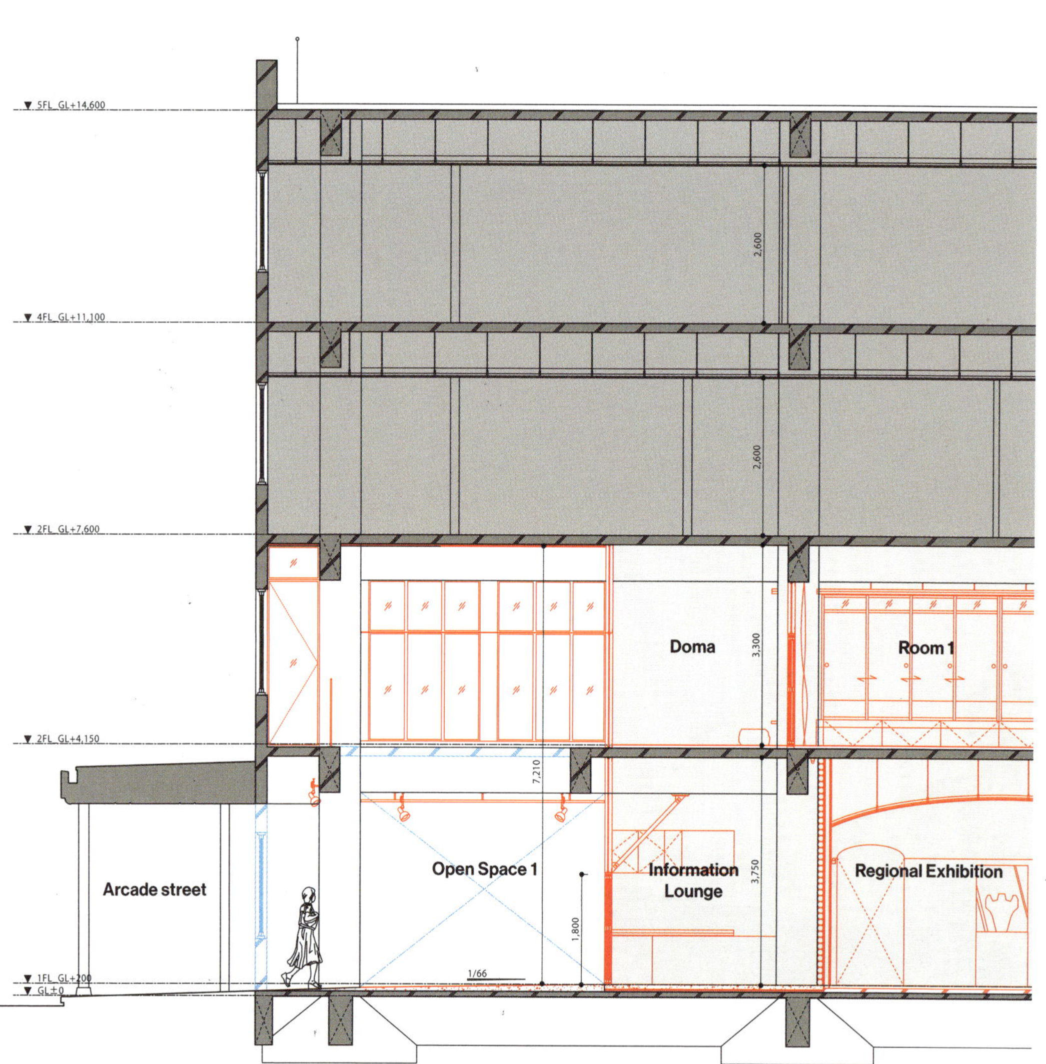

Sectional view of Bunjiro.

Existing Element

Newly constructed

Removed

Reinforced

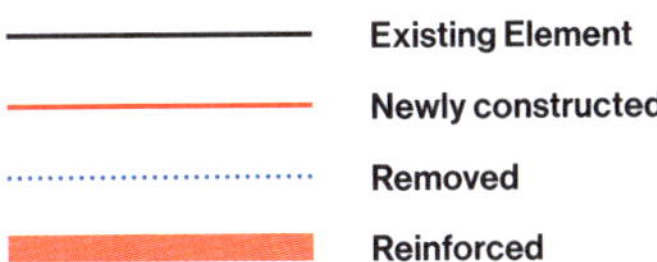

4FL_GL+11,550
3FL_GL+7,750
2FL_GL+4,250
1FL_GL+377
GL±0
300
3,500
3,500
3,873
Creation Space
Work Lounge
Open Space
Information
2/100

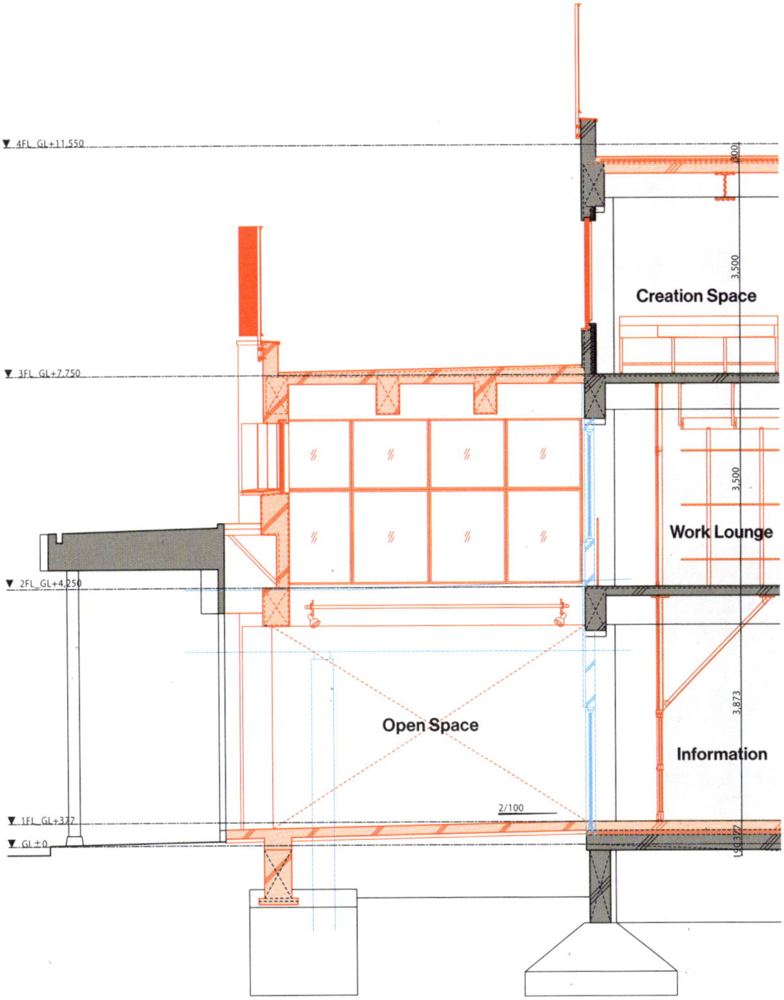

Sectional view of Jujiro.

As part of the downtown revitalization strategy, the architects proposed the creation of bright, semi-outdoor, multipurpose spaces on the margins between the buildings and the covered sidewalk. On the left is the Market Plaza, a semi-outdoor space. The brown wall is made of pressed *dorodango* mud balls handmade by local residents.

ております。
営業中

In Bunjiro, the glazing panel of the exterior wall below the height of 180 cm is made of wood and movable so that users can open the interior space into the external "marketplace."

Miyoshi Civic Hall Kiriri

DESIGN: AS
LOCATION: MIYOSHI CITY, HIROSHIMA PREFECTURE
COMPLETION: 2014

A public facility built with the risk of natural disasters in mind.

Top: The first floor sits atop five-meter-tall *pilotis* to provide an evacuation site for local residents in the event of flooding and to create a flexible open space that citizens can use for multiple purposes. Bottom: Because the Miyoshi area is known for its traditional performing arts, the main hall is designed with balcony seats projecting at right angles to the stage, as in a traditional Japanese theater. The hall can seat 1,006 people.

From the main hall to the studios, all rooms are connected by conspicuous corridors that make them equally accessible without any distinction between "front" and "back" areas. When major performances are held, the salon hall and all of the studios and practice rooms can serve as dressing rooms. The layout is designed to resemble a small town with various buildings lining the streets.

The foyer, with its panoramic views of the surrounding town, can be used for multiple purposes independent of the main hall's function.

Architecture with the Ordinary

Takahito Ito and Miho Tominaga

Manazuru, a town of some 6,500 people, is about an hour and a half by train southwest of Tokyo. It occupies the only peninsula to interrupt the otherwise unbroken arc of Sagami Bay, which stretches from east to west across the breadth of Kanagawa Prefecture. A flourishing port until Japan's early-modern period, Manazuru boasts a rich historical and cultural heritage. Its major industries are fishing, stonecutting, and agriculture, notably fruit. Today it not only supports people working in these primary industries but also serves as a bedroom community for city workers, and is a popular spot for vacation homes. While neighboring towns like Yugawara and Atami underwent development as hot springs resorts in the 1990s, Manazuru still retains the flavor of an old fishing village.

Since 2008, Japan has seen its population decline. In 2017, Manazuru, too, was designated a "depopulating area"—a rarity for a community so close to the Tokyo conurbation. However, two years prior, a certain couple had moved to Manazuru, burdened as it was by an aging, dwindling population and a lack of tourism resources.

This couple launched a project they call "a publishing house where you can sleep over." They made note of the differences between the urban environment they had previously called home and the unfamiliar place they were now living in—of the vibrant culinary traditions of the region, the rolling townscape with its proximity to nature, the energy that coursed through the town at election time, and the sense of belonging that came with an awareness of the importance of one's vote. They published books about the charms of the town and its lifestyle. And they offered accommodations and walking tours to people who came to see Manazuru, drawn by what they had read in those books. This cycle of information exchange is now bearing fruit in the form of new residents, new businesses, and new cultural amenities in Manazuru.

Initially, the couple had opened up a section of their house as an Airbnb, but then they decided to expand their activities by purchasing the vacant house next door and renovating it into a multiuse facility containing accommodations, a publishing office, and a book kiosk. They asked us, two people of the same generation, to handle the design work.

Are there constraints on the design of architecture in a place like Manazuru? The conventional wisdom has it that a big city offers ample resources, both human and material; a wealth of choices; and an infrastructure that ensures smooth access to them. In more outlying parts of the country, options are limited, access to goods and services sporadic. But once we embarked on our design project in Manazuru, we began to realize that such places offer another kind of architectural freedom and potential that one does not find in the city.

On a map of Manazuru, the architects noted the route of a walking tour (created and guided by the client) and the town's distinctive features.

Freedom on the Borderlines

Flanked by walls made of locally quarried stone and by the lush greenery of residents' gardens, the countless little roads that wind through Manazuru's neighborhoods are too narrow for cars to negotiate, but each pathway forms an intimate space for the people living there. The quality of such spaces is something that has been lost in the streets of big cities, where vehicle-friendly infrastructure takes priority. One of the challenges we faced was how to achieve this intimate continuity between the roads and architecture of Manazuru in our own design.

The lack of vehicular access poses a problem for fire and disaster prevention, but Manazuru seeks to ameliorate those risks through a volunteer firefighting brigade. The brigade also contributes to nurturing community spirit. It's a hallmark of cities to rely on impersonal outside services and institutions to address all the manifold risks of urban living. In Manazuru, however, architectural thinking need not rely on the existing infrastructure. Here one has the freedom to envision architecture in a context of loosely defined boundaries between houses, their surrounding gardens, and the infrastructure—a looseness predicated on interpersonal relationships.

Squeezing all the functions associated with "a publishing house where you can sleep over" into less than 100 square meters of space originally meant for family life was a unique renovation challenge, one that necessitated organizing these various functions in a mutually loose relationship.

At the harborside bar that served as a hub for interaction between old and new residents of Manazuru, the proprietor-customer relationship was loose in this sense as well. The owner played his guitar and drank with his customers, who reciprocated by helping clean up. This casual ambience, we thought, fostered a relaxed mood that encouraged people to relate to one another as individuals, without fixed roles or titles.

We wanted to take this idea of a space in which people were not constrained by clear-cut role assignments like proprietor and customer, but could reverse those roles at the slightest prompt, and apply it to the spectrum of spatial relationships extending from the road to the garden to the interior. Architects are normally expected to establish a hierarchy of "highlights" in the spaces they design, but for this project we chose to submit ourselves to the inspiration we found in Manazuru. Taking our cues from the intimate scale of the town's houses and their surroundings, we avoided creating any sort of hierarchy and instead sought to minimize the contrast between new elements and the ones already there.

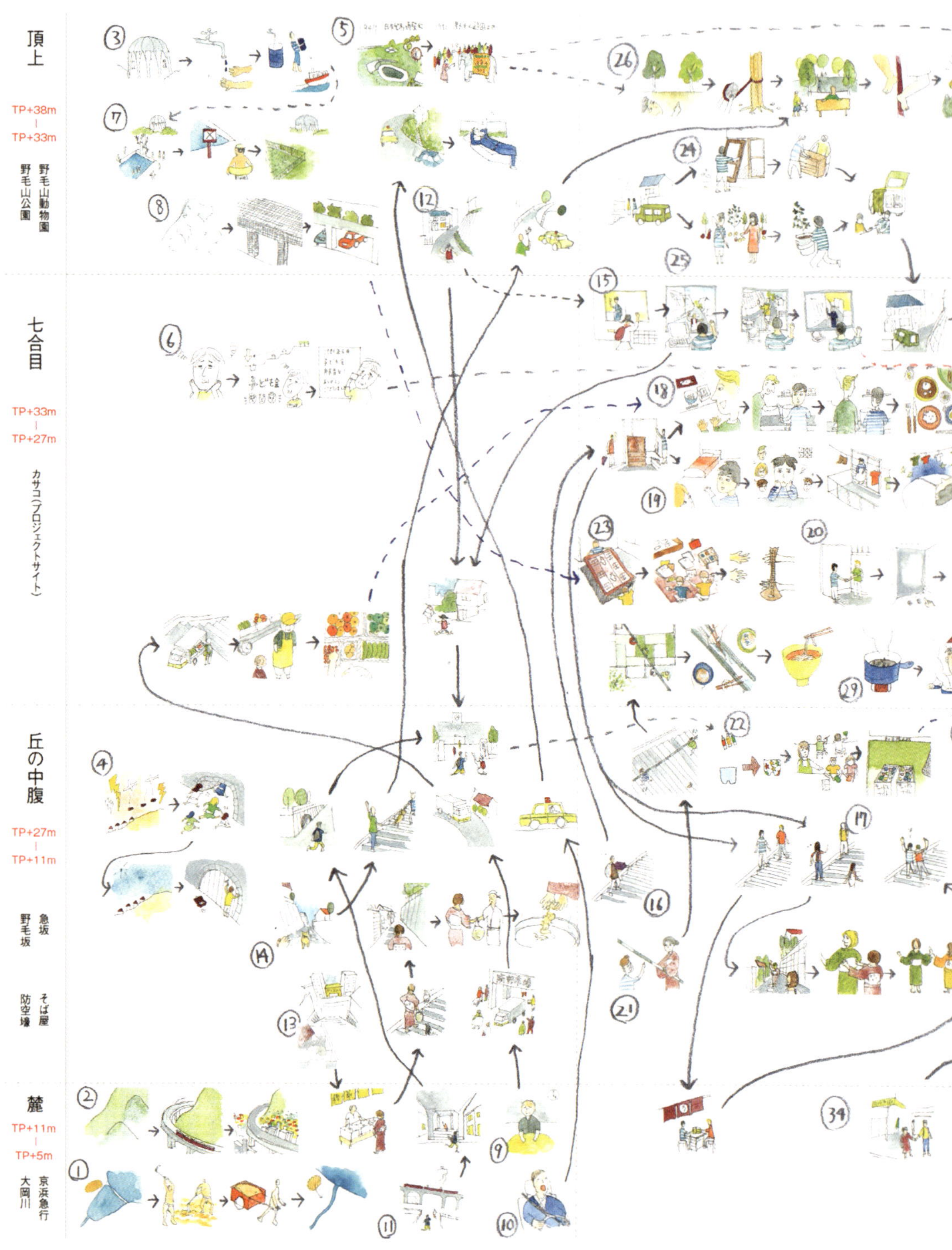

A local ecology map of Casaco, 2014–2016: When commissioned to renovate a house in a hill town in Yokohama, the architects collected townspeople's anecdotes, memories, and customs during the two years of the design process. Finding themselves drawn to the stories as fragments of an ecosystem, they then charted them on an X-Y axis, with X indicating time and Y the altitude on the hill. The ensuing chart provided an overview of the behaviors and activities of the residents (numbered in circles); the architects then added their proposed events, framed with brown lines. By drawing random lines between the existing events and adding new events, they tried to enhance this "ecosystem," and the ideas generated from this chart mobilized the townspeople to carry out some of the proposed events.

1.吉田新田ができるまで
2.京浜急行と地形
3.日本初の水道
4.防空壕が塞がれるまで
5.野毛山動物園ができるまで
6.子供会の消滅
7.プールが塞がれるまで
8.崖ガレージ
9.野菜の移動販売
10.丘の上のさぼりタクシー
11.麓の町から登校する
12.丘の上から登校する
13.そば屋の鰹出汁の取り方
14.犬の散歩
15.窓辺で作業する一日
16.麓の町で飲む
17.そば屋で浴衣の着付け
18.世界の料理の作り方
19.物干テラスの寝袋
20.WELCOME WALLができるまで
21.流しそうめん
22.ペットボトルキャンドル
23.軒先バザー
24.建具や家具をいただく
25.庭の苗木をいただく
26.スラックライン
27.坂の石畳が剥がされる
28.キャンドルナイト@急坂
29.ホットチョコレートの作り方
30.庭に畑をつくる
31.壁を取り、軒下をつくる
32.軒下に石畳を敷く
33.子供会の復活
34.野毛山動物園の帰り道
35.紙ヒコーキ工作教室
36.ランニングステーション
37.古タンスでカウンター
38.坂の猫の1日

ーン
移動
る出来事

Resources via Human Networks

Our Manazuru experience offered many surprises and discoveries in the realm of architectural resources as well. Architecture has become a highly industrialized field, so when we think about the windows or door handles for a house, we refer to the catalogs provided by manufacturers to check performance, design, price, and delivery time, and select appropriate products on that basis. During the design process we unconsciously rely on this industrial connection.

For the Manazuru project, however, we relied on connections cultivated in the course of the repeated "town walks" organized by Manazuru Publishing. When news came our way that the neighborhood post office was going to be torn down, we contacted the postmaster and obtained permission to work on the building for a few hours just before its dismantling. As a result, we were able to salvage a large aluminum window frame. When we were trying to figure out how much to pay for a front door handle out of the limited budget, someone we met at the bar suggested that we try recycling one of the broken anchors we occasionally saw lying by the harbor. We consulted with the friendly local dried fish shop, and the next day the anchor was delivered. The transmission speed of the human data network nurtured through those town walks proved to be faster than Amazon.

Accessing resources via industrial networks ensures budgetary computability and technical reproducibility, which a town-walk network cannot. But is that sufficient reason to exclude the possibility of reaping the bountiful fruits of "chance" from one's architectural calculations?

Reciprocity in Fieldwork and Design

Architectural practice today depends excessively on things that are computable and reproducible, while missing out on other possibilities that architecture ought, in principle, to embrace. This problem is linked to the relationship between fieldwork and design. As it is typically conceived, Fieldwork → Discovery → Design is a series of progressive stages in which "fieldwork" is defined as a process that derives certainty from uncertainty, providing us with something certain on which to base our design. However, defining "something certain" as "that which can be computed or reproduced" risks making this process an exercise in eliminating chance and otherness. To the extent possible, we should hold off on assigning meaning to our fieldwork exercises and keep the design process open to the randomness and otherness of events around us. This is, in fact, how fieldwork achieves its true significance. Ideally, fieldwork and design should always operate in parallel, constantly influencing one another in a reciprocal relationship.

Our experience in Manazuru gave us the opportunity to seriously contemplate what it is that sustains architecture, and what architecture itself sustains. Until then we had thought of rural Japan as a place that was blessed with proximity to nature but that did not measure up to urban environments in terms of infrastructure or in cultural and commercial opportunities. We assumed that people in such areas longed to live like people in the cities and were constantly striving to catch up with them; and no doubt many rural residents do think that way. However, this point of view derives from the values of industrial society, which we had unthinkingly internalized.

Our lives are sustained by industrial society: a powerful system that eschews the ambiguous, the uncertain, and that depends on reproducibility and exchangeability. Architecture, too, is inextricably dependent on this system. But in Manazuru, there is another kind of power, one sustained by a personal network of face-to-face relationships, that supports residents' livelihoods while allowing for the elements of ambiguity and chance inherent in them.

Architecture begins with the choice of which elements we tap for their power, and their potential to provide solutions to architectural problems. From that choice arises a dynamic reciprocal relationship in which architecture is supported by the power of those elements and supports them in turn. In rural communities, one can find a kind of power that has been preemptively eliminated from large cities and industrial society. When we incorporate that power into our thinking about architecture, it can have a liberating effect on our architectural concepts.

Manazuru Publishing Building 2

DESIGN (RENOVATION): MIHO TOMINAGA, TAKAHITO ITO (TOMITO ARCHITECTURE)
LOCATION: MANAZURU CITY, KANAGAWA PREFECTURE
COMPLETION: 2018

Walking up a stone-wall-flanked alley toward Manazuru Publishing Building 2. The tiny walkways that meander through the town's neighborhoods are known as *setomichi*—literally, "back-door paths," connoting their human-friendly aspect.

The architects drew successive images, like freeze frames, of the views along the two alleys on either side of the site, and used these sketches to study how to integrate this architectural addition into the landscape.

Manazuru Publishing Building 2 is a private home renovated to hold accommodations, a book kiosk, and a publishing office. Long-term visitors contemplating a move to Manazuru are welcome to stay here as well.

Top: The alleys of this intricate network serve both as walking paths across the slopes overlooking the Pacific Ocean and as neighborhood common spaces. Bottom: The large window facing the piled-stone retaining wall uses an aluminum frame retrieved from a dismantled post office. The architects designed the overall layout to provide a variety of comfortable "places to be" in the transitions between alley, garden, and house. Right: The designers made the interior as open as possible, maximizing its visual links to the outside.

The ambiguous space that forms a continuum from alley to garden to eaves to interior serves as the ideal gathering place.

Garden for a Second Life

Thirty years ago, some farmland in Sendai City was transformed into a housing tract of detached homes. The families that moved there at the time are now growing old. The architects devised a long-term scenario, one that would support the entire community, for an elder-care facility that sits on the border between the remaining farmland and the residential area. In this facility, incoming residents are encouraged to bring their garden tools, plants, and household furnishings with them to share as "community resources."

LANDSCAPE DESIGN: MIHO TOMINAGA, YASUMASA HAYASHI (TOMITO ARCHITECTURE)
LOCATION: SENDAI CITY, MIYAGI PREFECTURE
COMPLETION: 2020

The architects opened up the front yard of the elder-care facility and collaborated with its residents in creating a new garden landscape there, bringing all their plants and household tools together in one place. The garden is an intentionally ongoing project, an "unplanned ecosystem" that constantly changes according to the personalities and skills of the residents.

The garden accommodates gradual changes in the landscape as people from diverse backgrounds interact: neighborhood residents out for a stroll, children playing, senior citizens talking about their life experiences, people tending plants and flowers.

Gentle Development

Jo Nagasaka

Llove House Onomichi

When I stayed overnight at the Hotel Log in Onomichi in May 2019, I fell in love with a house I saw across the way. I immediately asked if it was available for purchase, and learned that it was over 110 years old. The house boasted a fine view of the Onomichi Channel stretching to the east and west, and was at an elevation just high enough to observe people walking on the streets at the foot of the hill. The panorama it offered of the town was perfect.

In 2021, I returned from a trip abroad and was required to self-quarantine for two weeks due to anti-Covid regulations. I decided to spend the time in this house, which had remained unused until then. Each morning I was awakened by the light reflecting off the surface of the Onomichi Channel. During the day, the islands of the Seto Inland Sea stood out in sharp silhouette, adding to the impression of the sea's breadth. At dusk the western end of the channel reflected the setting sun, and a refreshing land breeze flowed down from the mountain behind the house. Here, one could live while fully savoring the surrounding environment. I decided to buy the house.

Onomichi, however, is four and a half hours from Tokyo, even by the speedy Shinkansen. I doubted that I would find many opportunities to make use of the house myself. My real objective was to help preserve this beautiful landscape by giving others a chance to stay here and experience its pleasures for themselves. I began to develop plans for the Llove House Onomichi to be a "house for everyone," built with everyone's help. The aim of the project was to invite creators from all over the world—designers, architects, artists, chefs, musicians—to visit this lovely place, to express something about this town, and to communicate with it.

First of all, I needed someone who would run things locally in my absence. A married couple who are also my former staffers, Masami Nakata and Natsuko Matsui, volunteered to move here with their children. I entrusted them with overseeing the renovation work as well as the subsequent operation and management of the house. I also enlisted the help of Suzanne Oxenaar in the planning and curation work so as to ensure the inclusion of creators from overseas in our network. We obtained funds through the embassy of the Netherlands and a crowdfunding campaign, and members of the Tank design and construction team, along with local artisans and workshop participants, assisted with the actual renovation. Before we knew it, we had gathered a critical mass of interested, like-minded accomplices.

At the end of 2022, Llove House Onomichi began operating in a low-key manner. However, preservation of Onomichi's beautiful hillside environment will require more than just the success of Llove House Onomichi; the entire neighborhood also needs to be successfully preserved. To that end, it is important for Studio Basket, the office run by Nakata and Matsui, to actively engage

The architect removed most of the interior elements of the traditional Japanese restaurant that formerly occupied the space in order to produce a contrast between old and new.

with the community. Through the spaces and activities offered by Llove House, we want to work closely with our neighbors and utilize the expertise acquired through this project to help maintain and manage the local environment.

Matsumoto Jujo:
Complex of Tourists and Commercial Facilities

Asama Onsen, an old hot-springs resort in Matsumoto that peaked in popularity during the Showa era (1926–1989), has declined in recent years. The town is dotted with inns and hotels that are entirely closed off from the surrounding streets, so that even if these businesses manage to stay afloat, they do nothing to enhance the overall vitality of the town, which seems to only grow more desolate as its population ages.

Hotel proprietor Toru Iwasa, who runs the company Jiyujin, took charge of the revitalization of Hotel Koyanagi in Asama Onsen when he became president of the hotel. Iwasa developed a renovation plan that would connect the formerly enclosed hotel with the rest of the town. His vision was of a townscape enlivened by young couples from Matsumoto pushing baby carriages as they strolled the streets of Asama Onsen. We took on the task of "opening" the hotel to the town, and designed three facilities for that purpose.

1. "Philosophy and Sweets":
The First Step in Revitalizing the Town

This is a café just a one- or two-minute walk uphill from the hotel gate where guests can have their breakfast. We didn't want to ruin the nostalgic charm of the old house, so we renovated it with as few changes as possible. One distinctive feature is that the space has been stripped of most of its interior finishes, revealing the compacted earthen floor, on which we arranged furniture and built seating. We placed bookshelves at a bit of a remove from the walls, with seats behind them, forming alcoves in which customers can sequester themselves and read books undisturbed.

2. Asama Onsen Shoten:
Lifestyle Shop

We wanted this shop to be seen not as a souvenir outlet belonging to Hotel Koyanagi, but as a general store that would stand out among Matsumoto businesses. Our thinking was that this hot-springs district would require an image makeover if it wanted to regain its appeal to shoppers. The locale has a great many buildings that at first glance may appear dilapidated but that exude a special charm not found in the downtowns of cities like Tokyo. Places like this offer ideal opportunities for transformation by a younger generation of entrepreneurs. In that event, I hope there will be a demand for renovation designs that utilize the materials already on hand to the maximum extent feasible. Such projects may then provide the spark for larger-scale civic regeneration. In this case, I thought we could simply remove most of the interior elements of the Japanese-style restaurant that formerly occupied the space to create the skeleton. This culling process would produce a stimulating contrast between the remnants of the old wood-frame elements and the new reinforced concrete frame, giving the shop a distinctive air.

3. Koyanagi no Yu: Bathhouse

For many years the Asama area has had its own communal baths for local residents, but with the aging of the population, residents are no longer able to maintain these baths by themselves. We thought that by cultivating relationships over time with the operators of these baths and getting them to open up to the general public, including tourists, we could help make them a major draw for Asama Onsen. First, as a gesture of goodwill toward local residents, we decided to open a bathhouse at Hotel Koyanagi that emulated the compact, simple style of the communal baths.

However, this bath had to be an open-air one, so we designed a layout that would admit fresh air while minimizing the visibility of the interior from outside. We were also careful to select finishing materials that would resonate with those of other communal bathhouses in Asama Onsen, should they open to the public in the future. We used copper sheeting for the roof, added steam vents, built the outer walls of *sugi* cedar boards, and made the doors of transparent FRP (fiber-reinforced plastic) that would harmonize with the wood.

±0 Development

Does a place that has already modernized and enjoys access to all the necessities of life really need further development? That is a question I have been asking myself. At a time when environmental problems are on everyone's minds, Japan continues to pursue the kind of scrap-and-build development that provides certain conveniences at the expense of local character. Major train stations may boast about their unique features, but they are ultimately all the same. The construction industry sustains Japan's economy, so it is a hard habit to break.

One can, however, find intrepid souls in regional cities around Japan who are challenging this state of affairs. Among the examples I know of are entrepreneurs in mid-size cities like Fukuyama, Maebashi, and Niigata who are able to attract substantial funding for ambitious projects that exert a ripple effect capable of transforming the surrounding community. We have been fortunate to be hired to design some of these projects, and have gained invaluable experience working on them. Yet it is an undeniable fact that such projects sometimes seem excessive and detached from the reality of their communities.

Recently, though, one can also see less aggressive, more low-key efforts aimed at community resuscitation. There are people engaging in a barter-like economy on a small scale and living by values that sustain and enrich their lives, yet cannot be measured in cash. One exponent of this lifestyle is Goichi Miyamoto, who runs Chus, a market/dining/lodging facility in the mountainside resort of Nasu. By using the nonfat milk that is a by-product of the butter-making process at a nearby dairy farm to manufacture waffle cookies, he created a successful business that he then parlayed into the opening of Good News, a forest complex that includes a factory and a small shopping mall. The factory employs several hundred people on a very flexible schedule so as to accommodate employees with disabilities and housewives who can work only a few hours each day.

Activities like these contribute, however modestly, to the overall income of the locality. This in turn attracts quality shops from other places to open branches there, leading to the development of shopping malls where local people make purchases with their extra disposable income. Those profits cover the costs of maintaining the forest, thus supporting an entire ecosystem. By Miyamoto's reckoning, he logged one-fifth of his forest to make room for the mall and factory, but maintaining the rest has diversified the vegetation and preserved a rich natural environment that can coexist with human activity.

However small the scale, then, it is possible to gently upgrade a community while preserving its environment. By joining hands with neighboring communities instead of merely accruing know-how and profits within our own domain, we can build a finely meshed network. I am very intrigued by the potential of activities and networks of this sort to create what I call "gentle development." The social impact of such efforts is undeniable, but one of the tasks that awaits us is how to measure the value of that impact.

Llove House Onomichi

DESIGN (RENOVATION): JO NAGASAKA/SCHEMATA ARCHITECTS
LOCATION: ONOMICHI CITY, HIROSHIMA PREFECTURE
COMPLETION: 2022

The villa overlooking the placid Seto Inland Sea (above the concrete retaining wall at upper left) was renovated to serve as a "house for everyone." All the construction materials had to be hauled up and down the hillside via a steep stone stairway.

Above: Nagasaka's vision of "a house for everyone, to be built with everyone's help" was realized in collaboration with former staffers at his office, members of the Tank construction team, and artisans and workshop participants from the community. Bottom right: The living area on the ground floor of the renovated Llove House Onomichi. The renovation preserved the traditional furnishings that enhance the experience of sitting inside a house while enjoying the natural environment outside.

Top: Writing of the view from the second-floor sitting room, Nagasaka describes the morning light "reflecting off the surface of the Onomichi Channel to the east. During the day the islands of the Seto Inland Sea stood out in sharp silhouette, adding to the impression of the sea's breadth. At dusk the western end of the channel reflected the setting sun, and a refreshing land breeze flowed down from the mountain behind the house."

Matsumoto Jujo: Tetsugaku to Amai mono (Book Café)

DESIGN (RENOVATION): JO NAGASAKA/SCHEMATA ARCHITECTS
LOCATION: MATSUMOTO CITY, NAGANO PREFECTURE
COMPLETION: 2020

Matsumoto Jujo is a complex of tourist and commercial facilities designed to revitalize the run-down hot-springs resort of Asama Onsen. Schemata's mission was to carry out renovations that would "open up" the town.

"We didn't want to ruin the nostalgic charm of the old house, so we renovated it with as few changes as possible" (Nagasaka).

The interior of the book café seems like a natural extension of the gently sloping street outside. The leisurely layout of spaces feels contemporary.

Matsumoto Jujo: Asama Onsen Shoten (Lifestyle Shop)

DESIGN (RENOVATION): JO NAGASAKA/SCHEMATA ARCHITECTS
LOCATION: MATSUMOTO CITY, NAGANO PREFECTURE
COMPLETION: 2020

"We wanted this shop to be seen not as a souvenir outlet belonging to Hotel Koyanagi but as a lifestyle shop that would stand out among Matsumoto businesses" (Nagasaka).

What to remove and what to retain of the Japanese-style wooden elements: striking the right balance generates a sublime tension between old and new.

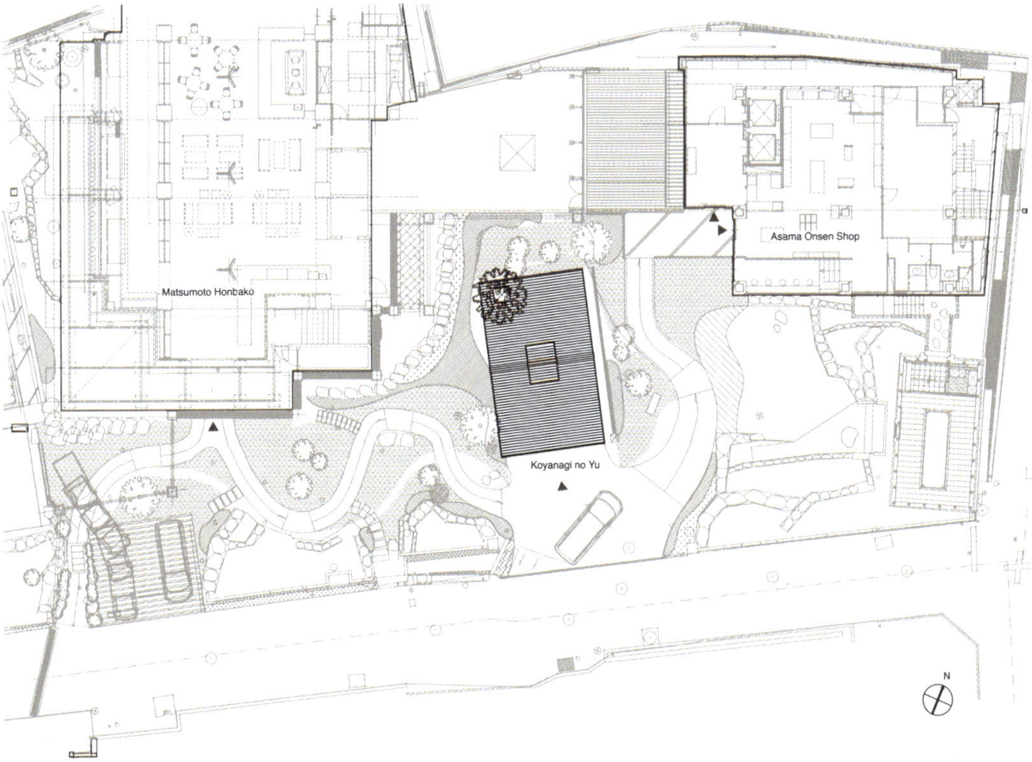

Top: Stripping away surfaces to highlight the beauty of the structure beneath is one of Nagasaka's fortes. Bottom: Next to the Asama Onsen Shoten sits Koyanagi no Yu bathhouse. Because it was planned as an open-air bath, "we designed a layout that would admit fresh air while minimizing the visibility of the interior from outside" (Nagasaka).

Matsumoto Jujo: Koyanagi no Yu (Bathhouse)

DESIGN (RENOVATION): JO NAGASAKA/SCHEMATA ARCHITECTS
LOCATION: MATSUMOTO CITY, NAGANO PREFECTURE
COMPLETION: 2020

Finishing materials for the bathhouse were selected to link its appearance to that of the older communal baths.

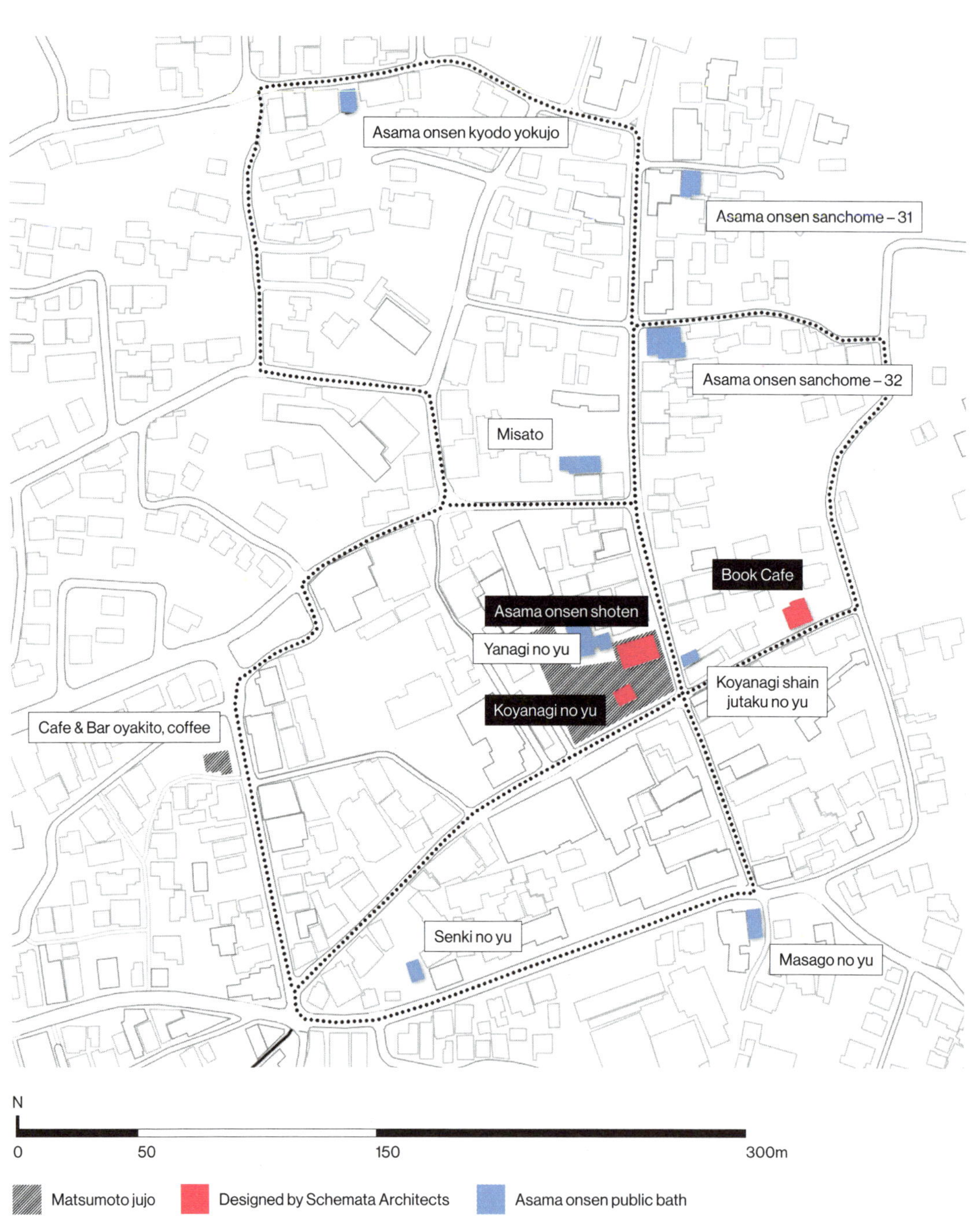

Asama Onsen once flourished as Matsumoto's "back parlor." Matsumoto Jujo is designed to foster a long-term future collaboration with the communal bathhouses scattered throughout the district.

Top: Though initially serving as a bathhouse for hotel guests, Koyanagi no Yu is also intended to lay the groundwork for the future opening of the town's communal baths to the general public. Bottom: The Koyanagi no Yu bathhouse design emulates the compact, simple style of the communal baths of Asama Onsen.

湯坂通り

3 Designing the Intangible

Community Design Encounters Population Decline

Ryo Yamazaki

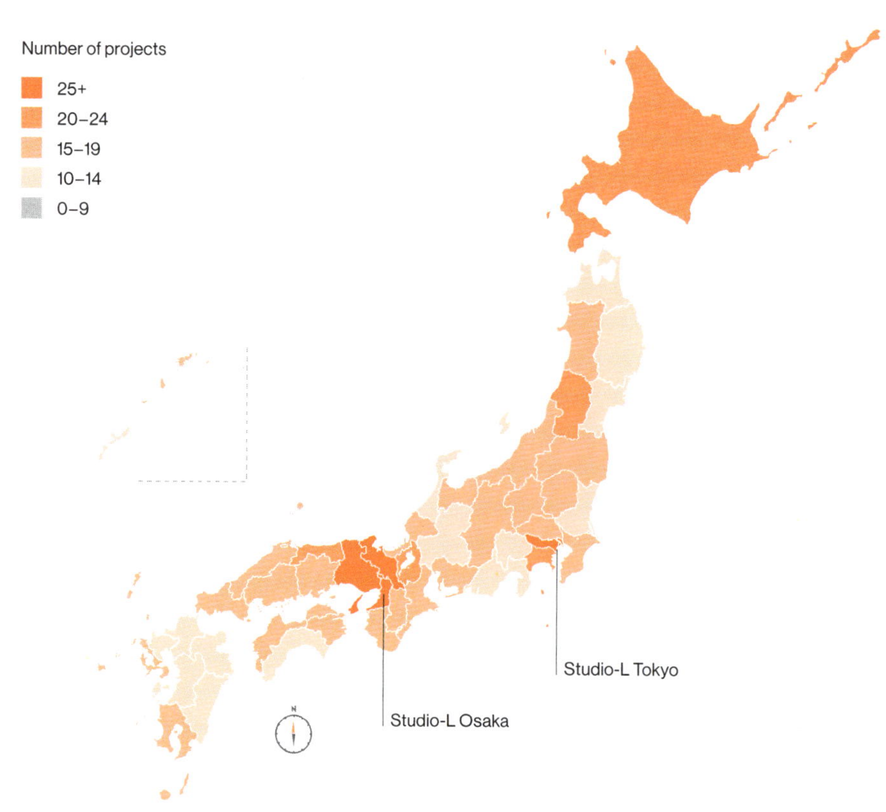

The number of projects (listed by prefecture) that studio-L, led by Ryo Yamazaki, has undertaken.

Since the 2000s, we've seen the rise of workshops that inform the design of public facilities, offering opportunities for extended dialogue between architects and the local residents who ultimately use their spaces. This is an achievement of community design. People in the field of architecture often ask me what new forms of expression this shift has enabled, but such an inquiry comes from a quintessentially architectural perspective. From the users' point of view, the impact on architectural expression is not particularly important. Rather, the far more relevant questions are, "How have our own thinking and lives changed as a result of the process?" and "What sort of relationships were formed or activities engendered?"

How has citizen participation in the design of public facilities, as mediated through community design, impacted design techniques? For citizens, what is the important part of the design process of public facilities, and how are local communities changing as a result? I believe architects with a proper grasp of these questions are more likely to discover new forms of architectural expression.

Public Buildings That Take Away Citizens' Opportunities to Learn

During the 50 years between 1950 to 2000, as Japanese society recovered from the war and achieved sustained economic growth, architects created numerous public buildings without engaging in dialogue with the public. We can describe this as an era when Japan filled up with public buildings that deprived citizens of the chance to learn. Architects imagined on their own how citizens they didn't know would utilize spaces; they relied on their own design logic and used philosophy to justify their designs. For the most part, citizens had little appetite for learning something new as adults and rarely considered what they themselves could do for the community, all while complaining about public buildings created by the government and architects.

It therefore seemed probable that the gap separating citizens and public architecture would never be bridged. Yet the work of community designers has helped to make the design process of public buildings less opaque. Workshops held before the architectural design process begins allow citizens to learn from one another about their lives and the future of the community, and they organize teams to implement the needed activities. Workshops also allow residents to define the conditions necessary to realize the vision of the community's future and each team's activities, and then reflect them in the parameters of the design competition. Architects who participate in the competition thus develop proposals based indirectly on the opinions of citizens. They also agree to participate in workshops and modify their proposals in response to further dialogue with citizens. Through their interactions with one another, architects and citizens learn about the design and management of the building.

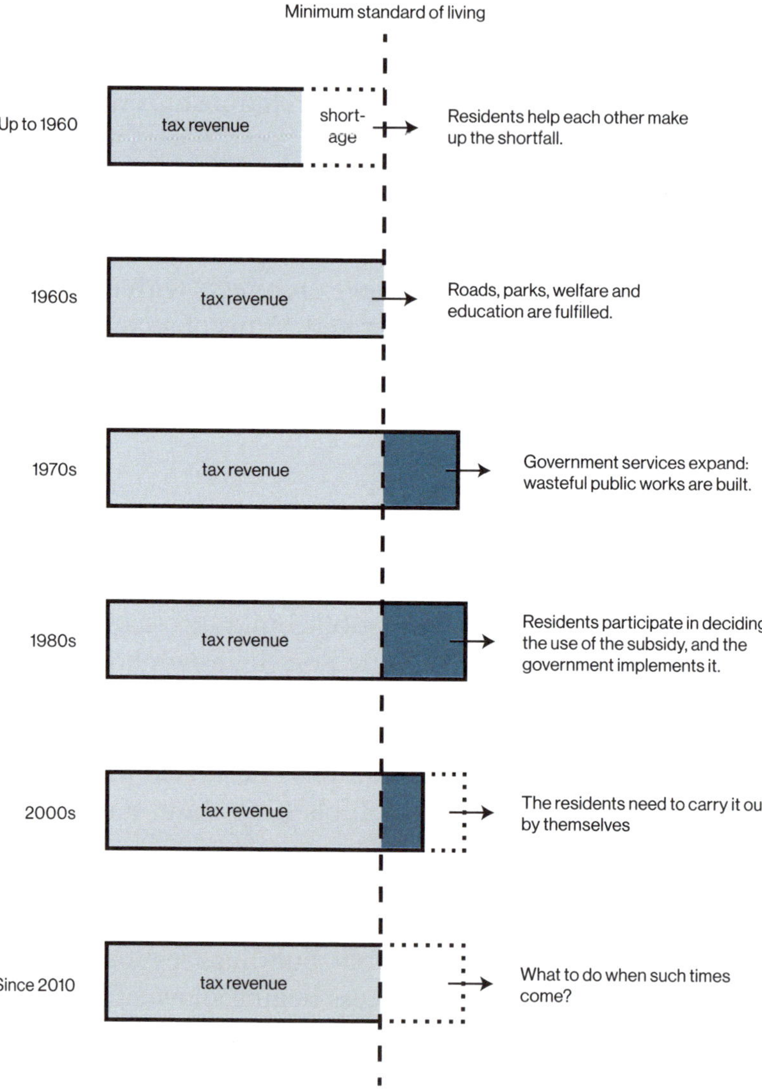
Tax Revenue and Administrative Services
Minimum standard of living
Up to 1960
tax revenue
short-age
Residents help each other make up the shortfall.
1960s
tax revenue
Roads, parks, welfare and education are fulfilled.
1970s
tax revenue
Government services expand: wasteful public works are built.
1980s
tax revenue
Residents participate in deciding the use of the subsidy, and the government implements it.
2000s
tax revenue
The residents need to carry it out by themselves
Since 2010
tax revenue
What to do when such times come?

Even so, the reality across Japan remained that most architects saw public commissions as a chance to use taxpayer money to create their own architectural works, and residents typically entrusted local governments with determining the future of their communities.

The Wake-Up Call of a Shrinking Society

However, around the turn of the millennium, Japanese society started to change in ways that called the meaning of public architecture into question. As the country's total population began to decline, local governments were confronted with a set of new realities:

(1) As population and tax revenues fall, the construction of new public facilities becomes either impossible or unnecessary.
(2) It becomes necessary to better utilize existing spaces as platforms for civic activities.
(3) Citizens are compelled to take responsibility for services that were previously the purview of local governments.

The transition of (3) is most difficult to accept. This is because people's mindset is shaped by the consumerist logic of society, which suggests that because citizens pay taxes, local governments should provide them with services, just as restaurants should provide food because customers pay for it.[1] This mindset also suppresses civic life. Services essential to daily life that were once provided through collaboration between community members are now something that residents pay corporations to provide. The need to pay for those services makes it difficult for citizens to cut down on their work hours. At the same time, many services that sustain local communities are provided by local governments, for whom citizens are vital taxpayers, which also prevents citizens from working less. As a result, more residents say that they do not have time to participate in community design workshops.

Community design has sought to push back against this consumerist mentality. The process invites residents to participate in workshops and shape their lives and communities through their own activities and dialogue, rather than rely on corporations and local governments to do so.

When (3) is achieved, residents soon develop a new sense of agency and community seems to reawaken. From a community design standpoint, the following changes begin to occur:

1 Here I distinguish between "citizens" who actively engage in a community and "residents" who only passively live within a community.

As a form of neighborhood revitalization, studio-L is helping the city and residents of Tachikawa City plan and operate programs for children at Tachikawa Kodomo Mirai Center in Tokyo (2013–present).

(4) Citizens learn from each other, build teams, and enjoy themselves as they begin to address local challenges.
(5) Renovation activities become more widespread and citizens become involved in actual renovation work.

When citizens learn from each other and their opinions are reflected in design, a wide variety of users make active use of new public facilities from the day they are completed. Ideally, facilities are staffed by community coordinators who encourage other citizens to use the facilities in ways both innovative and traditional.[2] After a few years, we should see citizens make the most of the space in ways that go beyond the architect's intentions.

At a workshop held for the design of the Tachikawa City Kodomo Mirai [Children's Future] Center, five groups proposed civic activities including "picture-story shows" and "manga talk battles." After the facility opened, the coordinators fielded many ideas from citizens, and six years later, the annual tally had swelled to 55 groups staging 376 activities, including purposes that were not intended by the architect, such as a center-wide mystery-solving game, barter events, and a traveling program on local shopping streets.[3]

Seeing Real Citizens

Young architects are also changing. Precisely because they are able to see the faces of proactively engaged citizens, I feel that more architects are able to interpret their role as simply enhancing essential factors such as structure, airtightness, and insulation, and offering spaces that actual citizens can make the most of.

In the days before workshops enabled direct relationships with citizens, architects' design process could be described in the following manner:

(1) Their own imagination of citizens defined the anticipated users for whom they designed spaces.
(2) They tried to find the human traits users had in common, drawing on anthropology and philosophy in their designs.
(3) They researched and applied design lessons from similar, already completed spaces.

However, when architects are able to see real citizens, new design techniques present themselves:

2 There are coordinators at many of the public facilities that we have been involved in.
3 The status of citizen activities at the Tachikawa City Kodomo Mirai [Children's Future] Center in 2013 and 2019.

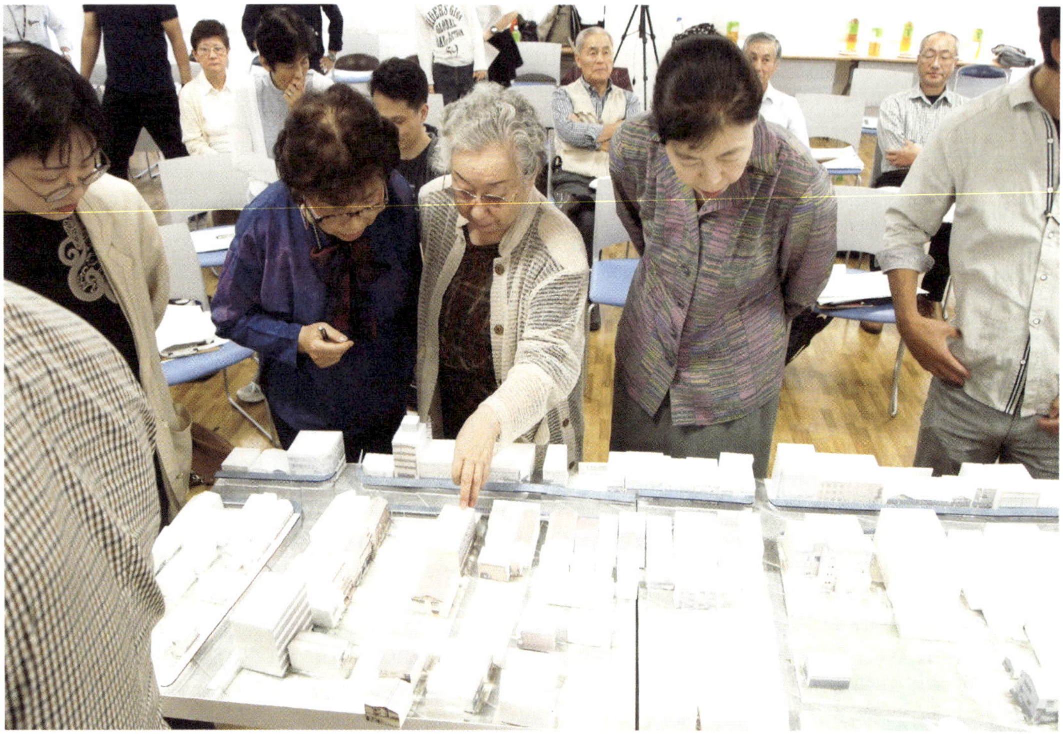

Top: From 2013 to 2016, studio-L helped the residents of Tokamachi City in planning and developing programs for two new platforms, renovated by Jun Aoki, in the declining main street (see pp. 70–79). Bottom: Prior to the start of the architectural design process by Kumiko Inui, studio-L helped the citizens of Nobeoka participate in planning the development of the central station area (2010–2015; see pp. 38–53).

(4) More free-ranging designs are possible, including adaptable or affordable spaces, based on the premise that workshop participants will be among the first users of the new building.

(5) In cases where a building has a resident community coordinator, spatial designs can go further in the direction of tolerance (i.e., can be used for any kind of activity) and ambiguity (i.e., assume that users will utilize the space in a variety of ways).

(6) In cases where workshop participants may be involved in the construction, choosing materials, methods, and forms that are amateur-friendly can cultivate citizens' attachment to the space and encourage them to imagine different ways to use it. In addition, bringing citizens into the construction process to perform repetitive tasks with small parts can make it possible to build spaces at a lower cost than would be incurred by solely relying on professional labor.[4]

Such design techniques may lead to the creation of novel spaces, but from the standpoint of citizens, participation in the design process promotes their agency, creates connections, and prepares a platform for activities, and *this is more valuable to them than the emergence of original architectural forms.* That an increasing number of architects truly *understand* this is a cause for hope. However, few architects are willing to *propose* a design process that presumes the agency of citizens. This is because architectural education still trains students to think of the client entirely as a customer. There is room for improvement in this regard.

Community Design without Community Designers

My hope is that someday the human bonds that once tied together local communities will be revived in new forms, and communities can develop without the need for community designers. If that happens, we can anticipate the emergence not only of geographic communities organized among neighbors, but also communities of interest where people with similar interests help and learn from each other beyond their local communities. Communities of interest will be enlivened by next-generation technologies and systems such as NFTs, smart contracts, and decentralized autonomous organizations based on the blockchain. The future coming into view is one of "community design without community designers." I dream of the day when this vision becomes a reality.[5]

4 At the citizen activity center in Tokamachi City, countless balls of mud packed by citizens were embedded in the interior walls to create a distinctive space (see p. 76).

5 Hints are likely to be found not just in technological advances, but also in local community management practices that used to be prevalent in Japan prior to the rapid population increase that began in the 1950s.

Top: The author's firm, studio-L, helped the citizens of Kusatsu City discuss the reuse of a former river site, come up with proposals for public programs, and participate in the design of a new public park over the site (2012–present). Bottom: During a workshop on the *ningyo-joruri* puppet theater in Chizucho, Tottori Prefecture, studio-L took the initiative of encouraging people in the Kansai region to learn about and participate in their traditional culture as a way of revitalizing the region (2014–present).

In Akita City, studio-L worked to enrich citizen communication, with a special focus on integrating the elderly community members and developing their role in transmitting the community's historical and cultural memory to the next generation (2018).

Top: A 2-km-long strip of vacant land was created after a railroad in the central Oita City was relocated. Bottom: Through seminars, discussions, and workshops, studio-L worked with the citizens as they participated in planning the reuse of the site as a public space (2012–2015).

In Uwajima City, studio-L is helping shopkeepers in a declining shopping arcade and local residents discuss and implement ideas for revitalizing the space as a large public park (2013–present).

4 New Strategies

Creating an Alternative Habitat Model

Yutaro Muraji

Commons for Habitat and Architecture, or CHAr, is an architectural startup focused on social change that launched in 2012. CHAr's mission is to deploy habitat models that answer the needs of the next generation. This requires that we architects and designers extricate ourselves from the structural constraints of the conventional contract model prevalent in capitalist societies (which has forced us into a subservient position relative to their clients) and instead actively identify and define social problems before taking the initiative to develop solutions.

The impetus for CHAr's mission arose from our efforts to solve problems associated with wooden rental apartment houses, the ubiquitous habitat typology seen in cities throughout Japan. Through the construction and implementation of a platform we call the Mokuchin Recipe [Ed.: *mokuchin* means "wooden rental," a slang term connoting cheap lodgings], CHAr has developed an architectural framework for its social mission and expanded the focus of its activities.

Mokuchin Apartments as Societal Resources

The wooden apartment houses that are the target of the Mokuchin Recipe designs are a standard building type that proliferated in Japan's cities after World War II. In Tokyo, the number of such structures peaked at 107 million units in 1973, when they made up nearly 30 percent of all housing units in the capital prefecture. These figures alone give a good idea of the tremendous impact wooden apartments once had on Japan's urban landscape.[1]

Mokuchin apartments were not public housing, but were privately owned and built by small- to mid-sized landowners. Their construction was not overseen by the national or local governments, nor were they designed by professional architects; landlords and the carpenters they hired built them in order to put surplus land to use. One might describe each of these structures as an autonomous aggregate of urban residential spaces.

Today, these mokuchin apartment houses are suffering the effects of Japan's population decline. This type of housing currently has a host of problems, including age and correspondingly poor condition, high vacancy rates, and the overall vulnerability to disaster they engender on a citywide scale due to their inadequate performance, which makes them a factor in the ongoing hollowing-out of Japan's regional cities.

On the other hand, mokuchin apartments are an integral part of Japan's back-alley neighborhood culture, the qualitative attributes of which cannot be recreated through planning. It therefore benefits us to ask whether it is wise to arbitrarily destroy these existing architectural and cultural networks through scrap-and-build redevelopment policies.

1 Byungsoon Park and Shuichi Matsumura, "Changes of Characteristics of Rental Wooden Multiple Dwellings in Tokyo," *Journal of Architecture and Planning* (Transactions of AIJ) 67, no. 553 (2002).

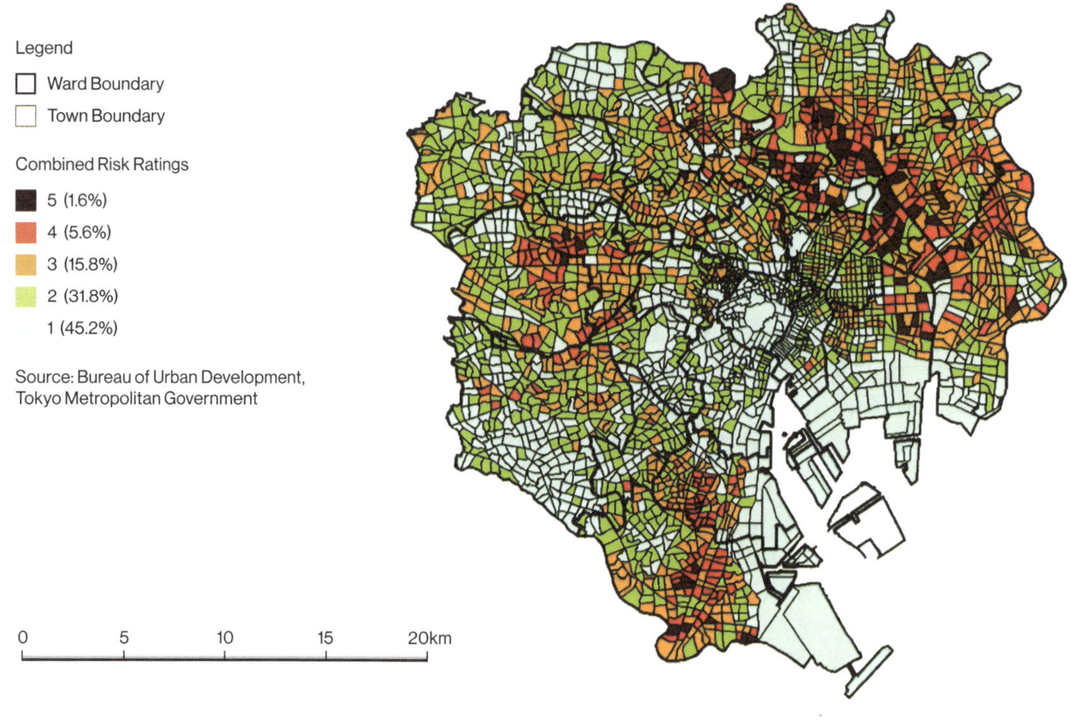

Combined risk ratings in the 23 wards of Tokyo, 2022. The "combined risk" means the total risk of buildings collapsing, fires breaking out, and the difficulty of activities during a disaster.

The mokuchin apartment is an architectural typology that has remained inaccessible to active intervention by architects, city planners, designers, and other problem-solving professionals. Nor has it been viewed as a design subject that merits intervention. The question of how to integrate this unsung resource into the social fabric so it can serve as a useful resource for society is a top agenda item for CHAr.

A Platform for Sharing Idea Resources

It is, of course, perfectly feasible for architects to resuscitate mokuchin apartments one unit at a time. However, such an approach would be ill-equipped to utilize the potential of the vast number of such apartments in this country. Our attempt at a solution is the Mokuchin Recipe web service, which we have been developing and operating since 2012. This is a design tool that freely distributes ideas, in modular yet universally applicable form, on how to repair and renovate mokuchin apartments. Users can create a renovation proposal by combining various ideas (or "recipes") from the site, and if they become paid members of the service they can download actual plans.

Mokuchin apartments share common layouts, dimensions, and components, so it is possible to apply a particular idea to multiple buildings. Our recipes permit many variations, ranging from simple, low-cost substitutions of parts to large-scale alterations that improve performance through earthquake proofing, modified layouts, and the like. The Mokuchin Recipe is updated monthly with user feedback; thus it is not simply a static and open source of ideas, but a dynamic system that is always evolving through user communication.

Most Mokuchin Recipe users are community-based realtors. The work of small- to mid-sized real estate companies in Japan includes handling management and tenant relations on behalf of building owners. In recent years these realtors have faced a number of challenges that threaten their profitability, among them the proliferation of real-estate brokerage sites run by large companies, increasing vacancies, and falling rental market values. CHAr's strategy is to effect community change in creative ways by improving the design literacy of local realtors through the Mokuchin Recipe service. These realtors possess robust networks with local property owners and other resources. If such players can be encouraged to take the initiative in creating added value for their communities, they will serve as a powerful engine of bottom-up change to their local landscapes.

To cite one example, the Heiwa Construction Corporation, based in Toda, Saitama Prefecture, has used the Mokuchin Recipe for over 80 renovation projects since it began partnering with us in 2015. Thanks to their repeated use of our recipes, the town has seen an increase in artists and other creators, a type of resident not previously found here. This has led the company

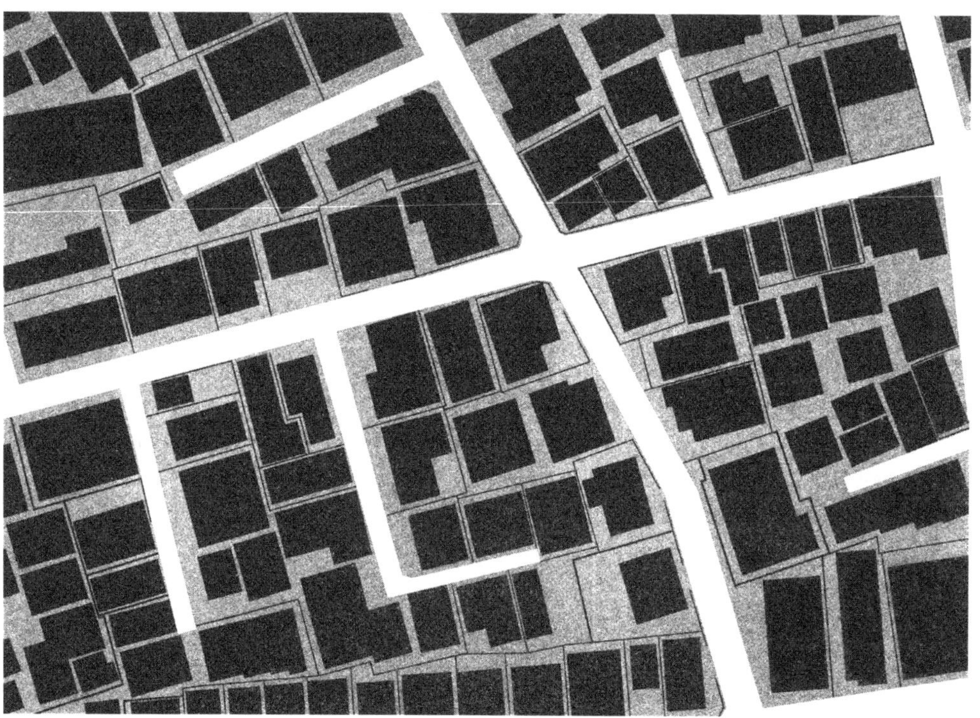

Top: Existing conditions: A typical urban neighborhood crammed with *mokuchin* apartment houses like so many closed boxes. The buildings look out on dark, narrow, dead-end alleys, isolating residents from the community at large. Bottom: Envisioned future. Expanding the use of Mokuchin Recipes can improve the connections between *mokuchin* apartments and their neighbors.

to embark with us on projects such as meet-and-greet events and the creation of new community spaces. These activities further accelerated when, in 2020, we jointly planned a new live-work rental house, named 2020/Feathers and Clouds, that would also serve as a community space. Today we are collaborating with nearly 30 real-estate companies like Heiwa, and nearly 100 users are renovating their spaces using the Mokuchin Recipe service.

Supporting a City with Commons

We have come to view our mission as the development of methodologies for using the Mokuchin Recipe to intervene in and renew cities through the propagation of new forms of information technology and creative thinking. Moreover, as a nonprofit organization, we have incorporated a social innovation framework that gained popularity in the last two decades and applied it to architectural practice. CHAr is also in the process of developing a new service in collaboration with other nonprofits. This is a community renewal model that will repurpose local buildings—not limited to vacant or newly built units—to provide a residential safety net for people in need, augmenting physical housing with comprehensive resident care and support.

In the long run, our objective is to overcome the model of architectural practice that increasingly locks architectural designers into a subservient relationship with their clients, a trend exacerbated by the growing influence of neoliberalism in our society. By taking the initiative in defining our sphere of activity and its significance, we can begin the process of identifying methods of achieving societal reform. The vision we see before us is the restoration of the spatial, temporal, and human relationships that have fractured and fragmented in the modern age. The new networks that arise will serve as a commons that will nurture habitats for future generations.

Mokuchin Method

STRATEGY AND DESIGN: YUTARO MURAJI AND EIJI KAWASE (CHAR)
LOCATION: TOKYO METROPOLITAN AREA AND OTHER URBAN AREAS OF JAPAN
COMPLETION: 2009–ONGOING

Normal

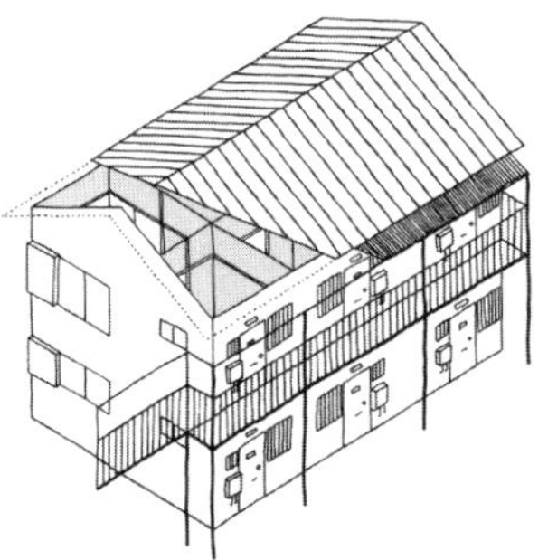

Long

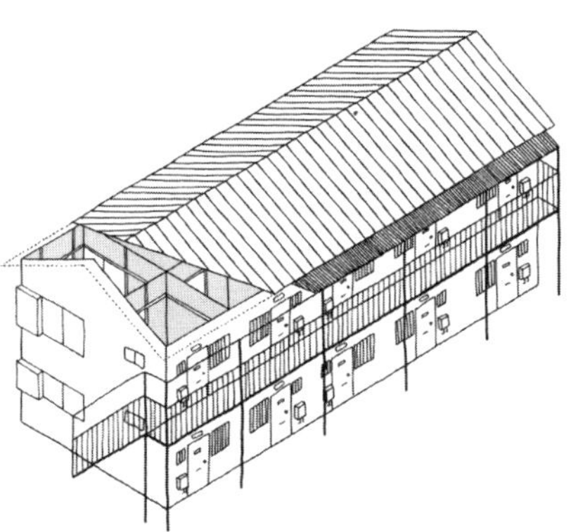

Fat

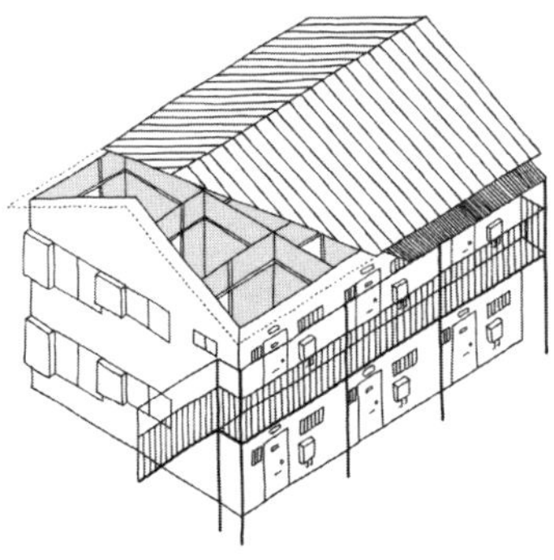

Mini

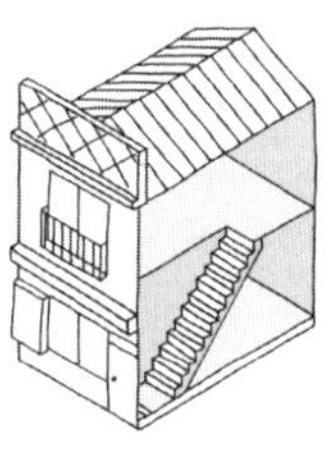

An overview of typologies of the *mokuchin* wooden rental apartment houses that Muraji and his colleagues have encountered in the course of their activities. The basic distinctions between types are in building length (i.e., number of apartments) and layout (how individual apartments are accessed).

Double

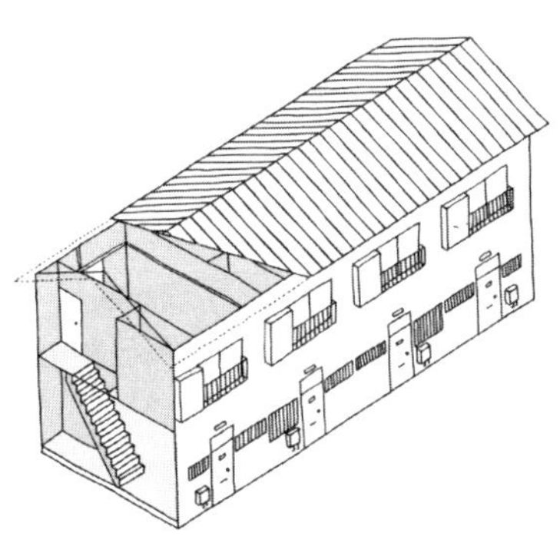

Sandwich

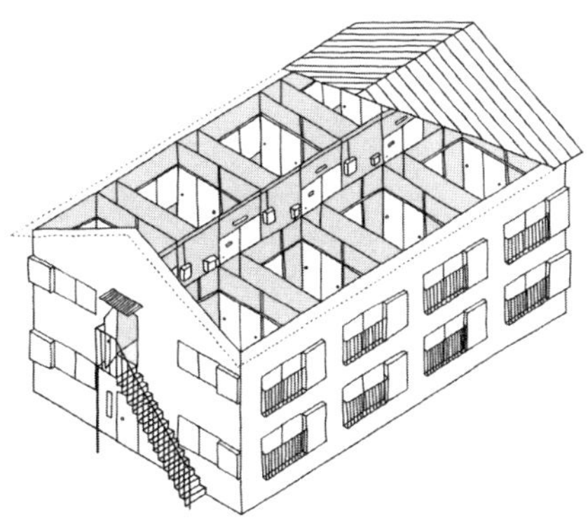

Winged

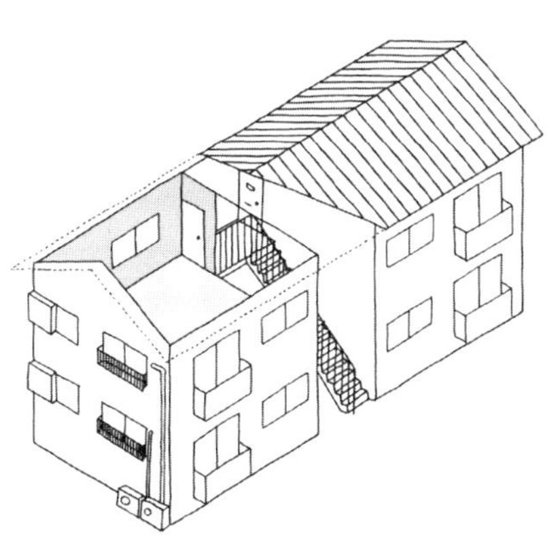

Mixed

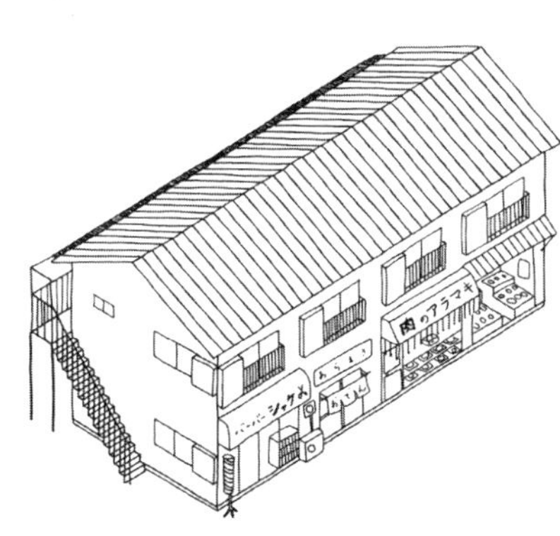

Zigzag

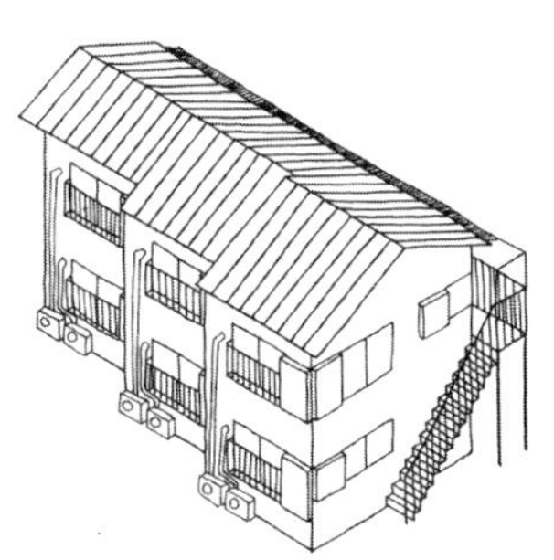

New Type

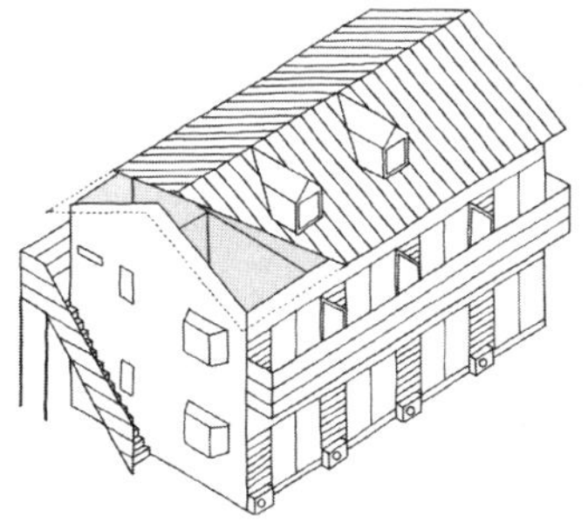

Mokuchin apartments rapidly proliferated in the late fifties, sixties, and early seventies, when there was a mass migration to Japan's largest cities. This type of housing could be built cheaply and quickly.

Mokuchin Recipe, the website launched by Muraji and colleagues, offers access to a vast trove of "recipes" for renovating wooden rental housing. Recipe items are designed for easy use by non-professionals, and the plans can be downloaded after paying a membership fee.

Kubomi (Ota-ku, Tokyo, 2017): A small wooden building in a commercial district was converted into a gallery with the use of four Mokuchin Recipes. The curved interior wall has the visual effect of bringing the street right into the building. The creation of this common space will hopefully give some stimulus to a shopping area that has seen better days.

Top of this and facing pages: From First II (Kawasaki, 2011). Six recipes were used to improve a *mokuchin* apartment house that was typically lacking in privacy, sunlight, and ventilation.

Bottom of this and facing pages: Pin! Hirahirabashi (Yokohama, 2017). Ten recipes transformed a dark, cluttered outdoor corridor into a pleasant interface with the surrounding environment. The newly inset space provides room for bicycles and planters.

Wings and Clouds (Hane to Kumo)

DESIGN: CHAR
LOCATION: TODA, SAITAMA PREFECTURE
COMPLETION: 2020

CHAr pursues alternative forms of development, as in this example of a new *mokuchin* apartment house designed in partnership with a local real estate company in a Tokyo suburb. Each of the three live-in units has a studio facing the street, encouraging interaction between residents and the community.

The unit adjoining the terrace can be used for community events.

不動産
○○○不動産

An urban neighborhood of the future that nurtures human connections, as envisioned by CHAr. Social safety nets can be expanded not only by renovating *mokuchin* apartments but also by converting vacant apartment houses into common spaces where people in the community can help one another.

A World in Which Anyone Can Be a Creator

Koki Akiyoshi

We launched the architecture-related startup VUILD in 2017 with the aim of realizing a world in which anyone can be a creator. Since then we have developed roughly four businesses with the mission of liberating people's inherent creativity.

The first area is the sale and distribution of CNC milling machines in forested mountain areas throughout Japan. So far, we have introduced these machines in over 150 locales. Our second project facilitates online orders for the processing of wood products via a nationwide network of these milling machines. Our third project empowers people to build their own original houses by utilizing this production and distribution network. The fourth area is the carrying out of innovative architectural projects utilizing this system and platform.

Restoring Autonomy through Forestry

The initial impetus for these undertakings was the Great East Japan Earthquake of 2011, which made me aware of the limitations of our country's centralized political and economic system, a factor that contributed to the Fukushima nuclear plant accident and the inability to respond to the tsunami that followed the earthquake. I became interested in the possibilities of developing a more autonomous, distributed production system as a solution to those limitations. Then it occurred to me that the ultimate state of autonomy in architecture or city planning might be achieved by empowering everyone to use familiar materials to create the environment of their choice with their own hands. That, I thought, would also bring about the ultimate state of sustainability, peace, and happiness. This line of thinking led me to focus on wood, a plentiful resource that can be obtained anywhere in Japan, where trees cover two-thirds of the nation's territory.

When I began to immerse myself in the world of forestry, however, I soon discovered a host of problems. First, forestry was not a profitable line of work. Second, forest resources were not utilized in an efficient manner. The main reason for this was that forestry communities lacked the means to process their wood locally. Though they could produce the raw material, they could not convert it into meaningful products. Since they only sold lumber as-is, they were forced to market their product on the cheap. The solution would be to add value to that product, and I thought that digital fabrication would serve this purpose well. Digital processing machines are inexpensive and easy to operate; introducing them to these communities seemed like an effective way to reinvigorate their local industries.

In the past, communities like these had plenty of master carpenters who knew how to process wood locally. However, as architecture became increasingly industrialized and production more centralized, small communities lost

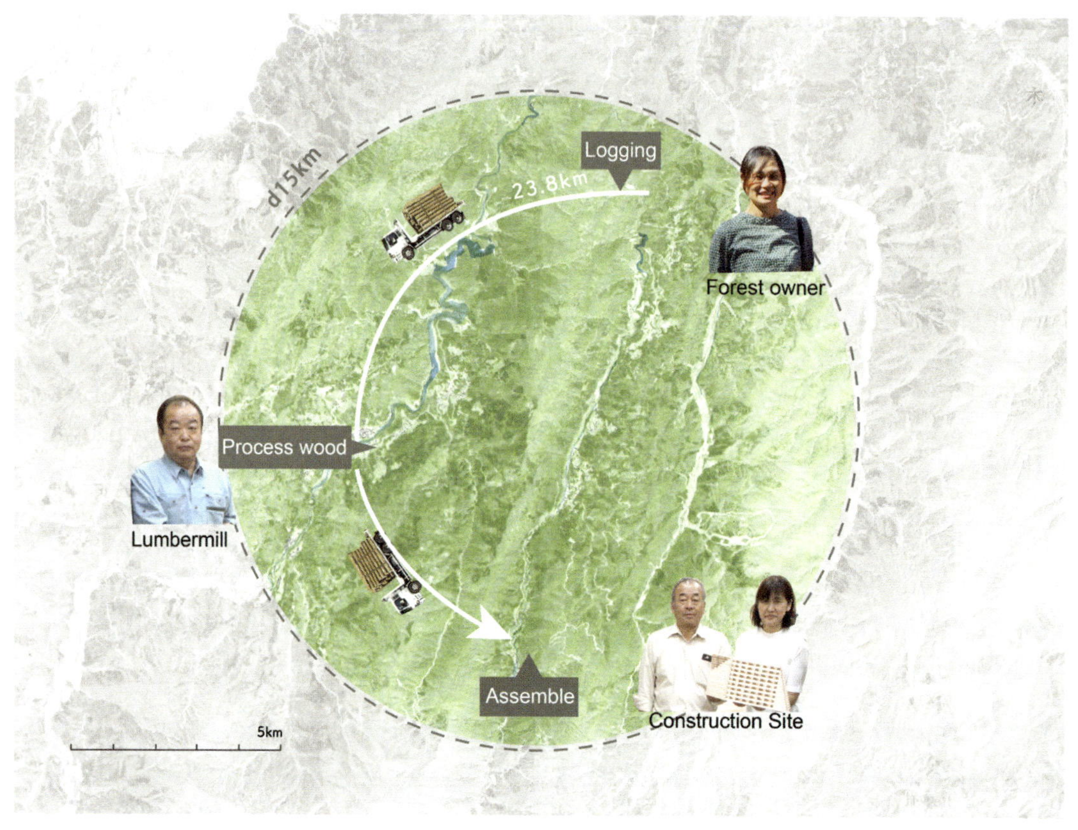

VUILD's proposed autonomous distributed forestry system. All steps, from lumber procurement to construction, are carried out within a ten-kilometer radius. The House for Marebito was built using a network that meets this requirement.

their autonomy. Today, lumber meeting certain specifications is shipped in from all over the country and precut at large mills to the standards stipulated for conventional wood-frame house construction. This industrialization of wooden housing contributed significantly to the amelioration of Japan's postwar housing shortage, but it also accelerated the nationwide standardization of the construction industry and thus weakened industries on the local level. By restoring an autonomous distributed system to these communities—this time through the use of digital fabrication—I thought it would be possible to revive their local industries. And in the process it might restore the local roots of architecture as well.

Locally Produced, Locally Consumed

While entertaining this idea in my mind, I visited Toga-mura, a depopulated village in Nanto, Toyama Prefecture. The region is known for its traditional farmhouses in the *gassho-zukuri* style of steep thatched roofs, which are jointly built and maintained by members of the community. This tradition stems in large part from the area's geopolitical history as a place of exile cut off from the rest of the country, a situation that forced its inhabitants to sustain their living environment on their own. But this also meant the region remained largely untouched by Japan's wave of industrialization, making it the ideal place to test the potential of digital fabrication as a means of giving new life to the local housing industry. That is how we came to build an inn, House for Marebito, in collaboration with the local residents we got to know over the course of frequent visits to the area.

For the design, we attempted to create a contemporary version of the traditional *gassho-zukuri* style using a method of construction that could be accomplished with a low-cost CNC milling machine. Each element was composed of members no more than 30 mm thick and one meter long so that anyone could participate in the construction work, just as with the *gassho-zukuri* houses of old. We also succeeded in carrying out all the steps from tree felling to construction within a ten-kilometer radius, thereby demonstrating the validity of a "locally produced, locally consumed" process that required no long-distance transport of materials.

The House for Marebito thus represents the realization of our vision of applying technology to the revival of local industry and culture, a vision achieved through the fusion of digital fabrication and traditional building techniques.

House for Marebito

DESIGN: VUILD
LOCATION: TOGA VILLAGE, TOYAMA PREFECTURE
COMPLETION: 2019

Nestled amid mountains that rise to over 1,000 meters, the village of Toga-mura is in deep-snow country, and 97 percent of its land is forest. The village's population began to decline during Japan's era of rapid economic growth; today only about 500 people live there.

Marebito means a "visitor from afar" who has a powerful impact on a community. Akiyoshi and his colleagues felt that the village needed an influx of both visitors and residents in order to solve its depopulation problem. As a pilot project, they built House for Marebito, a shared cottage for short-term stays.

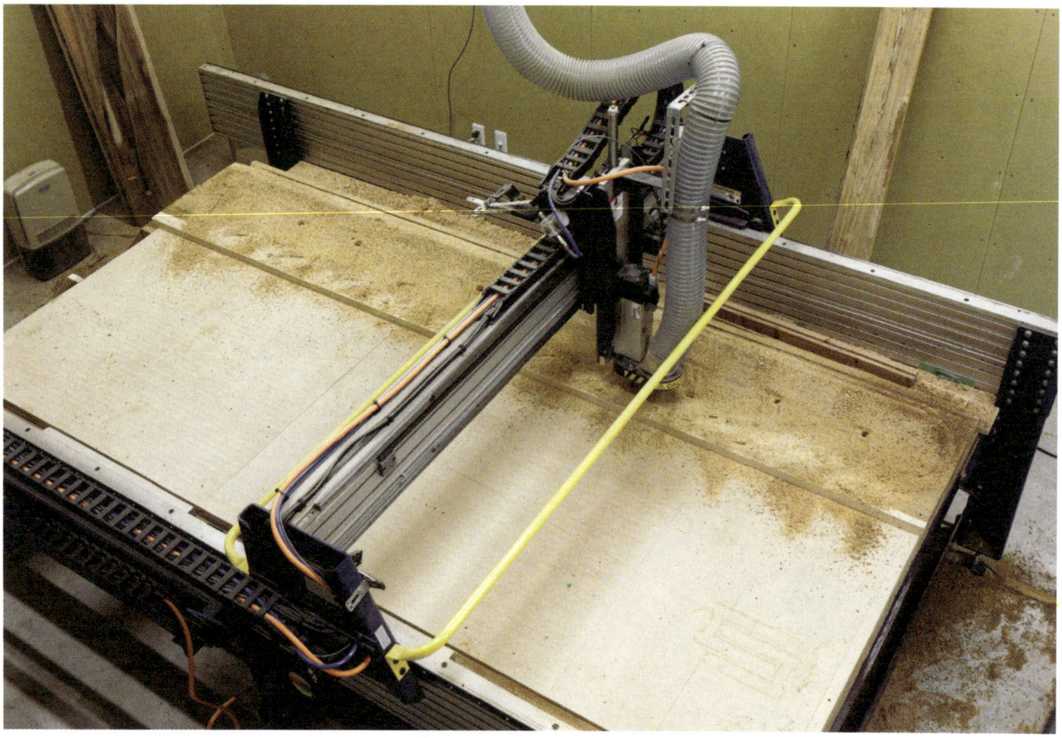

Wood members cut by a ShopBot CNC milling machine were assembled entirely by joinery without the use of any metal fittings.

After studying *gassho-zukuri*, the area's traditional building technique, Akiyoshi and his team developed the contemporary digitally fabricated version of construction.

Left and center: Sunlight penetrates the interior through apertures between the beams that form the east-west facade. Some of the windows are rotated to function as windcatchers. Right: The house design utilizes contemporary technology to recreate the steep-roofed *gassho-zukuri* style house traditionally found in snow country. The exterior is covered with *sugi* cedar bark shingles, as is common with farmhouses in Japan's colder climes.

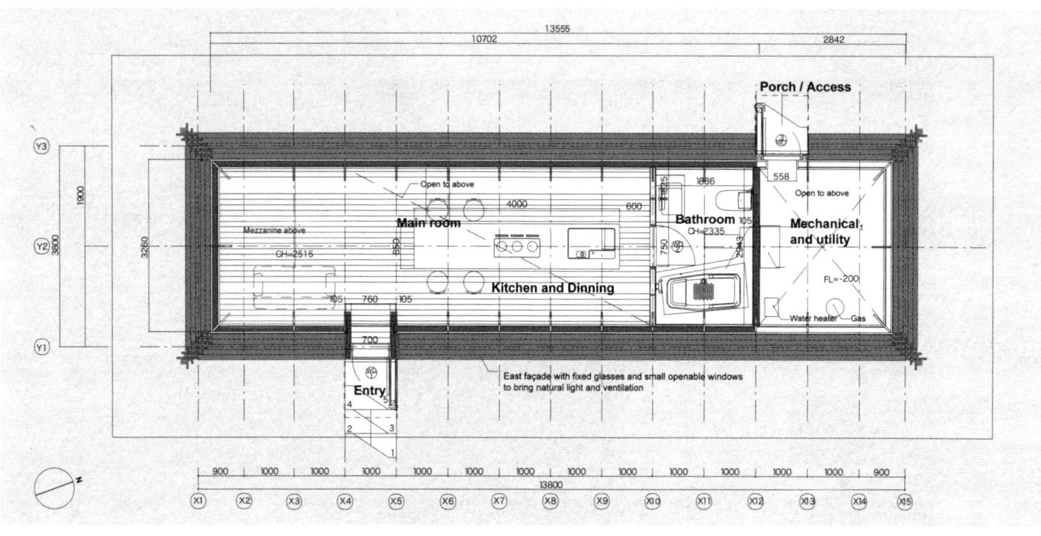
13555
10702
2842
Porch / Access
558
Open to above
Open to above
1886
4000
600
Main room
Mezzanine above
CH=2515
850
3260
1900
3800
Bathroom
CH=2335
750
Mechanical and utility
Kitchen and Dinning
FL=-200
Water heater
Gas
105
760
105
700
Entry
East façade with fixed glasses and small openable windows to bring natural light and ventilation
900
1000
1000
1000
1000
1000
1000
1000
1000
1000
1000
1000
1000
900
13800
X1
X2
X3
X4
X5
X6
X7
X8
X9
X10
X11
X12
X13
X14
X15
Y1
Y2
Y3

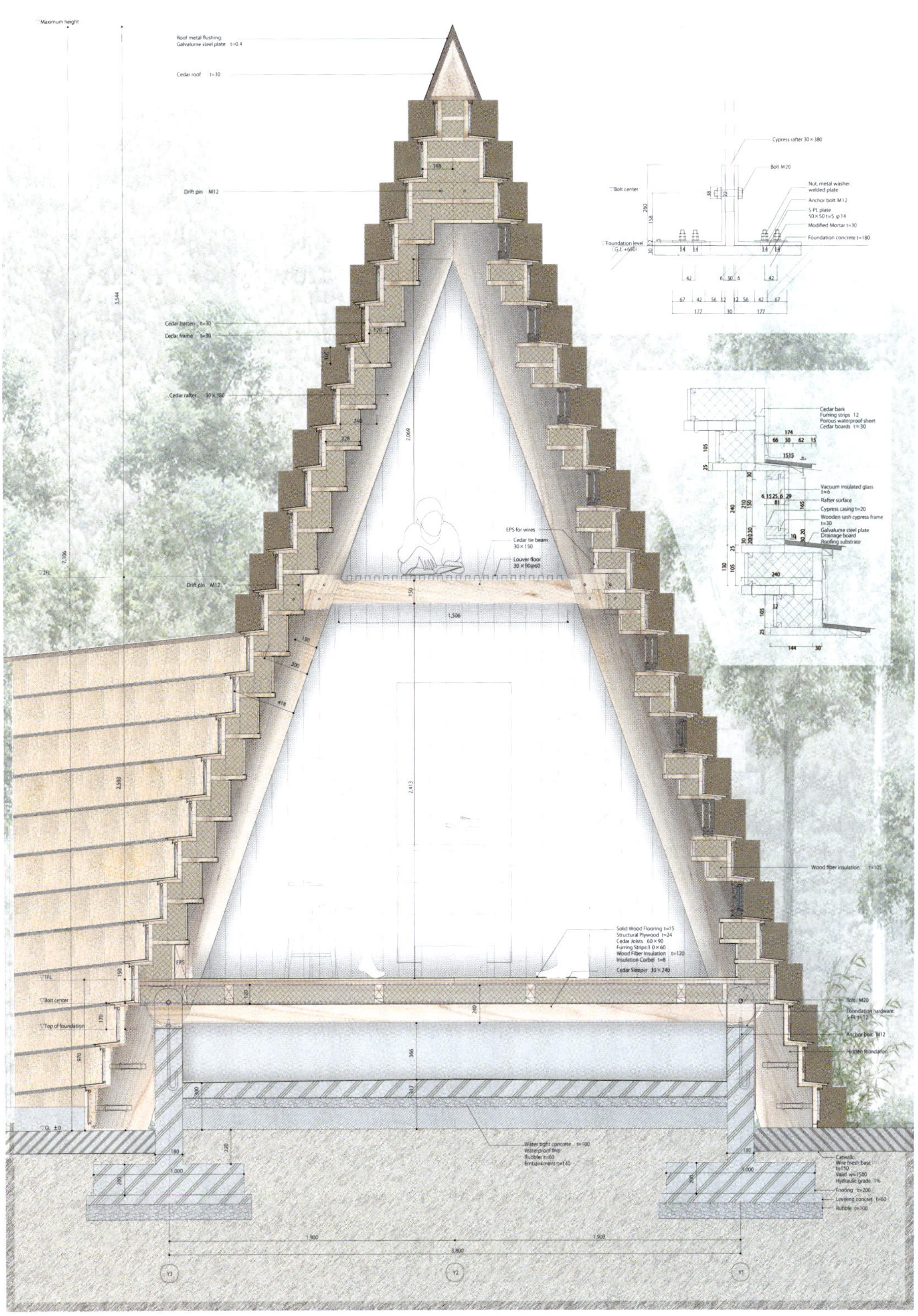
Maximum height
Roof metal flushing:
Galvalume steel plate t=0.4
Cedar roof t=30
Drift pin M12
Cedar batten t=30
Cedar frame t=30
Cedar rafter 30×380
EPS for wires
Cedar tie beam 30×150
Louver floor 30×90@60
Drift pin M12
Cypress rafter 30×380
Bolt M20
Bolt center
Nut, metal washer welded plate
Anchor bolt M12
S-PL plate
Modified Mortar t=30
Foundation concrete t=180
Foundation level
Cedar bark
Furring strips 12
Porous waterproof sheet
Cedar boards t=30
Vacuum insulated glass t=6
Rafter surface
Cypress casing t=20
Wooden sash cypress frame t=30
Galvalume steel plate
Drainage board
Roofing substrate
Wood fiber insulation t=105
Solid Wood Flooring t=15
Structural Plywood t=24
Cedar Joists 60×90
Furring Strips 3.0×60
Wood Fiber Insulation t=120
Insulation Corbel t=8
Cedar Sleeper 30×240
2FL
1FL
Bolt center
Top of foundation
GL ±0
Bolt M20
Foundation hardware
Anchor bolt M12
Hidden foundation
Water tight concrete t=100
Waterproof film
Rubble t=60
Embankment t=140
Catwalk
Wire mesh base t=150
Footing t=200
Leveling concret t=60
Rubble t=100
Y3
Y2
Y1

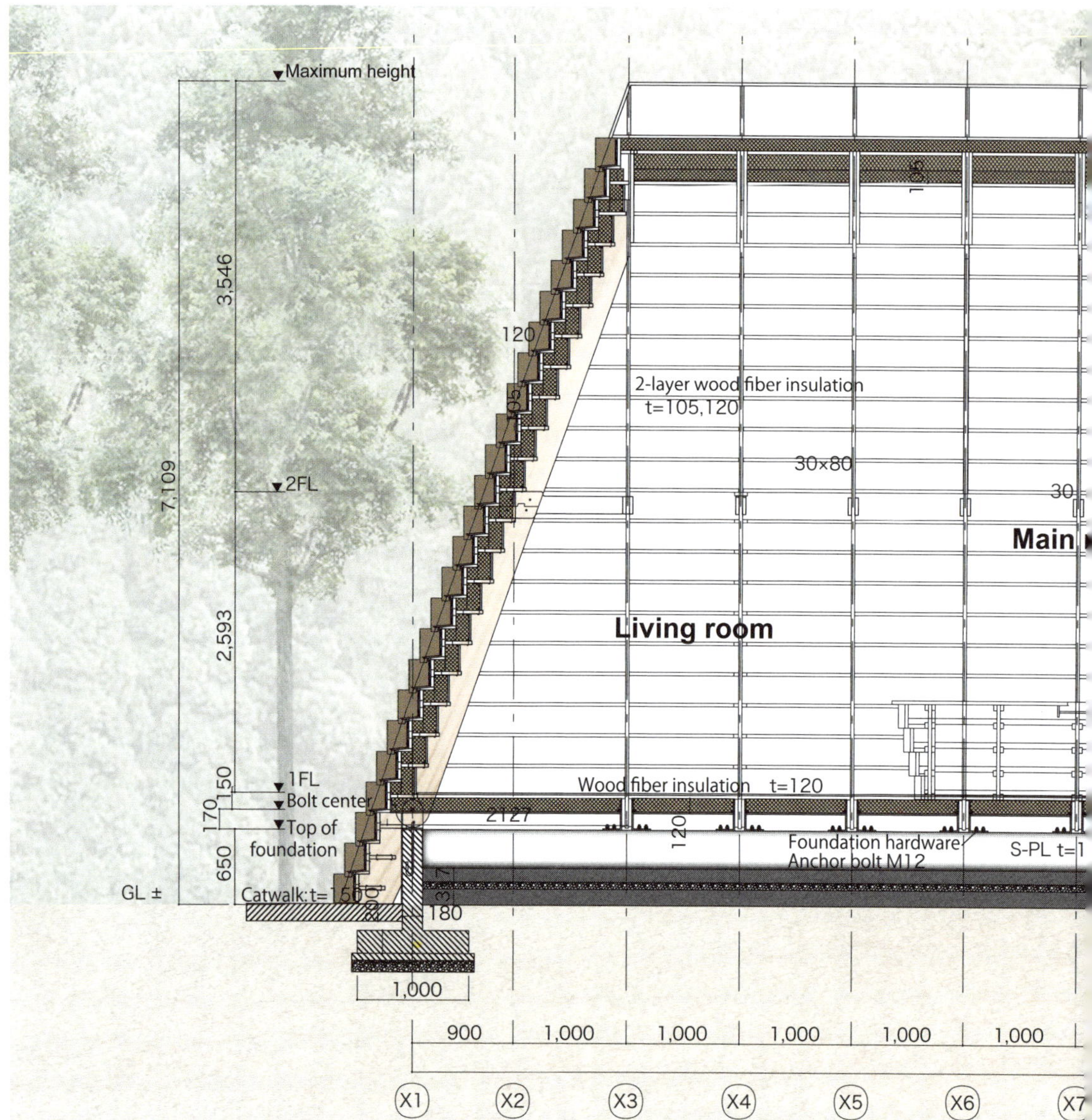
Maximum height
3,546
7,109
2FL
2,593
150
1FL
Bolt center
170
Top of foundation
650
GL ±
Catwalk:t=150
120
2-layer wood fiber insulation
t=105,120
30×80
Main
Living room
Wood fiber insulation t=120
120
Foundation hardware
Anchor bolt M12
S-PL t=1
180
1,000
900
1,000
1,000
1,000
1,000
1,000
X1
X2
X3
X4
X5
X6
X7

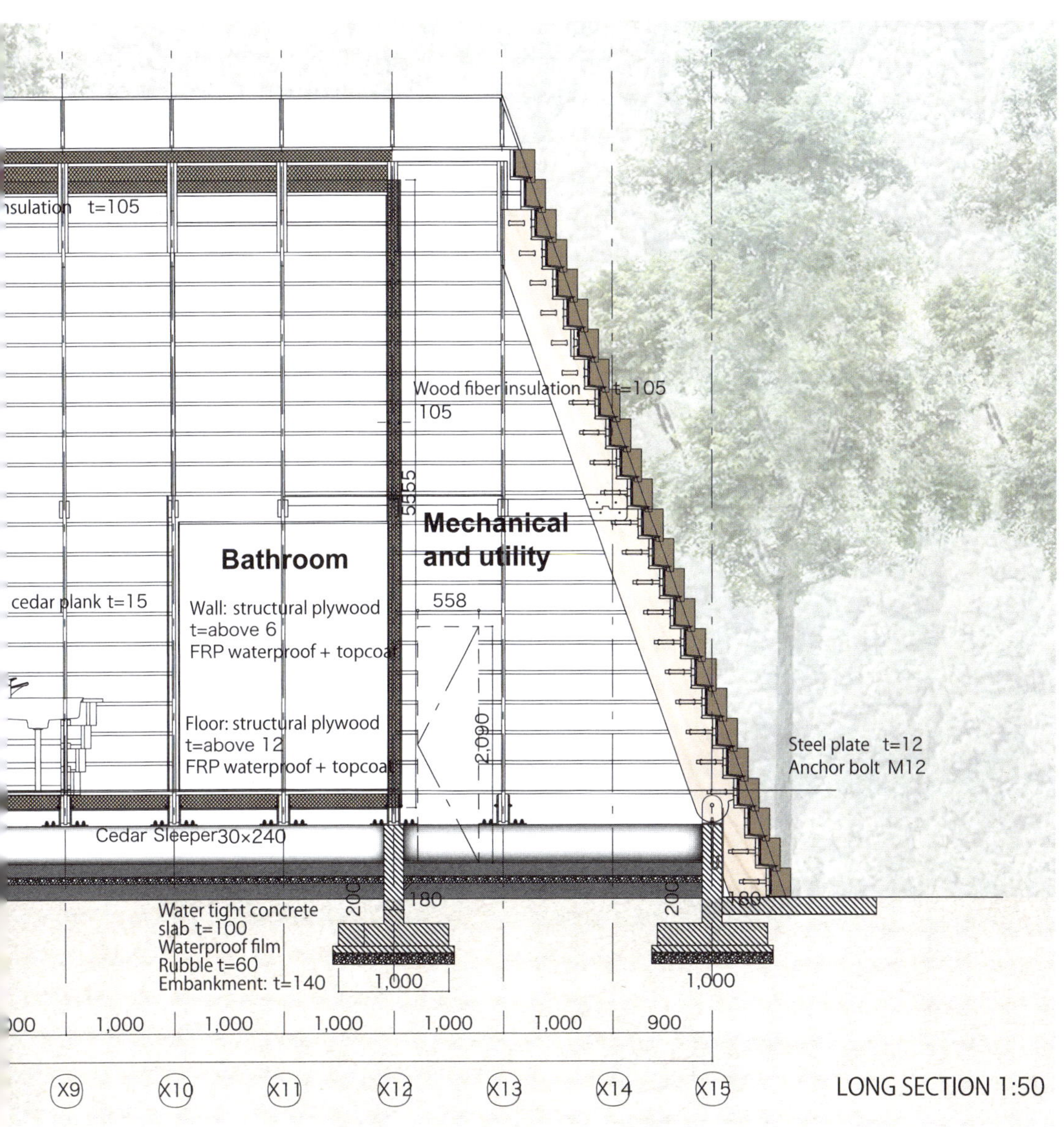

LONG SECTION 1:50

The house can sleep up to six people. Everything—from the building itself to the kitchen furnishings—is made of 30-mm-thick *sugi* board. The insulation packed into the walls was also made of wood fiber.

5 Documentation

Onomichi: The State of Things

Kenta Hasegawa

CYCLING ROAD

ミハルスポーツ
センター街
あぃさーQ
センター街
マサヤ
センター街
まさ吉
ノルディック・ウォーク
HATACHI
カラオケ
どれみ
そば
うどん

たこ焼
たこすけ
センター街
中川硝子店
センター街
ヤマダヤ
センター街
大本呉服店
センター街
VISA
VISA
裏地
ボタン
木曽ラジオ
センター街
センター街
センター街
シミズ
センター街
はんの専門店
小岡印房
モリシ
JCB
はん

と 24

尾道市
土堂二丁目
2
Onomichi-shi
Tsuchido
2-chome
2

孔雀荘
珈琲

らくれん

寺道踏切
221k198m

道具

~みんなの願い交通安全~
交通安全推進事業所

YASHINOMI

ボン

光明寺
西土堂

Open
Close

井上家之

管理番号:広405
(ニシゴショ)
西御所アンダー
大雨時
冠水注意
緊急連絡先
尾道市 維持修繕課
TEL:0848-25-7273

村井くだもの店

4

よう！
3
尾道市立大学
3
新尾道駅
BUS
4
新尾道駅

BUS
9
4
桜土手

桂馬
石畳小路
靴下専門の店
マサヤ

GOOD TASTE
COFFEEBOY
清春
刃物

フレンド
株式会社はせべ

土堂シティマンション
P
24時間OPEN 20分/100円
桂馬パーキング
定休日
です

E.Kinashi
福山誠之館

36

防犯カメラ
作動中
ALSOK

しまなみ信用金庫

HOME CENTER
ユーホー

6 Projections

Agents of Change

Mohsen Mostafavi

Onomichi is a port city dating back to the medieval period in Hiroshima Prefecture, the western part of Japan, with a history of shipbuilding. The city was also one of the main locations for Yasujiro Ozu's 1953 film *Tokyo Story.* In Ozu's film, the slow and gentle life of Onomichi is contrasted with the pace of modern Tokyo when an elderly couple makes the long and arduous trip to the capital to visit their grown-up children, who have little time for them and show little respect for their traditional values.

The contrast between Tokyo and Onomichi is still evident today. The population of the latter has been gradually declining over the years: currently around 130,000 people, it is expected to fall well below 100,000 in the coming decades. Onomichi is typical of other small Japanese cities experiencing the stark consequences of demographic change, from an aging population and a low birthrate to depopulation and a lack of local and easily accessible resources such as supermarkets and health clinics. By contrast, in larger cities like Tokyo or Osaka, the signs of demographic change are less visible, masked by the size of their population that is, in part, supported by migration from other parts of the country. In time, however, even the larger cities will no doubt be impacted directly by demographic change.

Because of its scale and history, Onomichi provides a valuable case study for addressing demographic change and, more specifically, the question of whether the spatial transformation and revitalization of smaller towns can create incentives for both local inhabitants and internal migrants. With good ferry links to several nearby islands, Onomichi has gained a reputation as a scenic area for holidaymakers, bicycle tourists in particular. New opportunities like this have become an important part of the city's identity as it makes the transition from its traditional role as a port town/shipbuilding region and tries to attract a younger generation of migrants from other parts of Japan.

One of the benefits of visiting a small city such as Onomichi is the relative ease with which one can become familiar with the physical characteristics of the area. Equally valuable are the benefits of meetings and conversations with the residents. During a recent trip, I was able to meet with several younger residents who had moved or returned to the city relatively recently. One is the young architect Ami Ishihara, who decided to relocate from Tokyo to Onomichi in the reverse of the young characters in Ozu's masterpiece. For Ishihara, working in Tokyo had become associated with design projects for anonymous clients and, to some degree, locations. She felt that working in a metropolitan context made it difficult for her to experience the direct and immediate consequences of an architectural project on the local community.

Ishihara had worked for Jun Aoki in Tokyo for several years. While there, her responsibilities included being the architect in charge of an observatory that Aoki's office had designed on top of the hillside in Onomichi. It was during one of her many site visits that Ishihara began to consider the benefits of moving there. She felt that living in Onomichi would allow her to meet new people and work closely with her clients as well as provide her with direct access to her project sites. Her decision may seem adventurous and risky; however, the research and preparation she carried out during her visits to the city increased her chances both of working with the city administration on small public projects and finding private clients.

Ishihara is part of a younger generation of Japanese professionals who consider moving to a small town to be a rewarding experience, one that allows them to craft a more meaningful lifestyle and make a more tangible contribution to their local communities. For Ishihara, new architectural projects have also become a vehicle for closer collaboration on a building's purpose. In her new role, she feels able to make programmatic suggestions that can be of greater service to the client as well as to the context. This type of engagement between the architect and the client may be uncommon within the confines of conventional practice. In many ways, Ishihara feels that her role as an architect in Onomichi moves beyond that of a mere service provider into greater participation in the life of the community.

Masako Toyota is an activist and entrepreneur who gained a great deal of experience working and living in Osaka (as well as traveling to other countries) before returning to Onomichi, where she was born. She now runs an advisory service for those interested in acquiring and remodeling abandoned homes. She has also developed several for-profit projects, including an unusual building called Gaudi House, which she and her carpenter husband renovated into a vacation rental. For Toyota there is no conflict between her entrepreneurial projects and her role as someone interested in the social and economic revitalization of Onomichi; the one supports the other. Her entrepreneurial activities help sustain social initiatives that in turn result in employment for others.

It was the rebuilding of an abandoned home that brought Natsuko Matsui, a publicist, and her architect husband, Masami Nakata, to Onomichi. They had both worked for the celebrated architect Jo Nagasaka of Schemata Architects in Tokyo before leaving to establish an independent practice in Nakata's hometown of Nagano. But they were tempted by Nagasaka's invitation to move to Onomichi to supervise the restoration of an abandoned house, one on a hillside with beautiful views, which Nagasaka had fallen in love with during a visit. Now known as the Llove House Onomichi, the building will host creators from all over the world who came to spend time living and working for a limited period in Onomichi. During the first phase of the project, Matsui is helping with a collaboration formed between Nagasaka and the art director Suzanne Oxenaar to bring Dutch artists to Onomichi.

For Natsuko Matsui and her young family, living on the Onomichi hillside is a deliberate choice that is not without its challenges. Typical everyday things that can be taken for granted in other places, such as easy access by public transport to medical care or a local supermarket, are made more complex by the relative inaccessibility of services. Yet Matsui and her family have made a commitment to stay, and both she and her husband plan to establish their careers in Onomichi.

These three women are agents of change. Each is an outsider (though Masako Toyota was born there) who has made the conscious decision to move to Onomichi and contribute to the next phase of its evolution—and improvement. Even in contemporary Japan, the situation for women can be harder than in other developed nations. These young women possess the commitment and dedication to their endeavors to produce imaginative and successful outcomes. Onomichi needs more such figures in order to deal positively with the social and spatial consequences of demographic change. In the meantime, these three women of Onomichi will play their part in safeguarding the city, revitalizing the community, and rebuilding for the future.

Revitalizing Onomichi: The Iterative City

Mohsen Mostafavi and the Studios at the Harvard Graduate School of Design

"Revitalizing Onomichi" was a research design studio conducted during the spring of 2023 at the Harvard University Graduate School of Design. The programmatic aim of the studio was to explore the intersections between architecture, urbanization, and demography in the context of a typical Japanese regional city today. How might architecture and urban development provide alternative social and physical frameworks in response to demographic change? Can a more subtly calibrated set of architectural interventions create a reimagined urban fabric between the old and the new, one that is perhaps also an antidote to the typical and at times devastating implications of large-scale development?

In the projects shown on the following pages, architecture—and, more broadly, design—is used as a means of transforming the city. To achieve this task, a series of multiscalar programmatic interventions are dispersed in various parts of Onomichi. These proposals are intended to enhance the quality of life of the inhabitants and to overcome some of the urban challenges brought about through aging and depopulation.

Studio model in which the proposals are incorporated, displaying a partial view of central Onomichi's seaside.

The approach of these projects differs from that of conventional urban design: they aim to produce greater compactness and densification through their number, size, and proximity to each other and to other facilities in the city. The relationships between the newly proposed structures and those already present form an important component of the proposed revitalization strategies (as well as their potential future adaptability). This iterative city is made up of an evolving series of initiatives, activities, and functions for both young and old, as well as for the hillside and the downtown. The designs invariably reconsider the status quo by juxtaposing programs and exploring their in-between characteristics and unexpected relationships.

The proposed programs range from educational and cultural buildings to communal and shared structures and spaces. Their functional span is also broad, encompassing the provision of food and produce for the elderly residents (who find it difficult to climb the steep hillside steps with their shopping) and a new ferry terminal (with a café and boatbuilding facility) connecting the town to the nearby islands. An important challenge for cities like Onomichi that simultaneously face depopulation and degrowth is how to address the increasing number of abandoned houses, empty lots, and urban voids. Can these hollowed sites provide new opportunities for the city and its citizens? Can degrowth lead to new ideas and new architectures that can simultaneously help sustain the existing community of Onomichi and create opportunities for in-migration?

This series of projects offers both reflections on and responses to these questions. In the process, each project demonstrates how the effective transformation of a city is contingent on both public and private engagement and cannot be left solely to the benefits or vicissitudes of private development. Each has grown out of a pedagogical experiment in rethinking the relationship between architecture and urbanization in an unfettered way.

Close-up view of the model showing the different proposals in context.

Productive Voids
Hugh Taylor

How much, and what, should we build in a post-growth condition? This project investigates the productive potential of voids. Two projects—one a brewery, the other a funicular—are organized along two lines between the hill and the seaside. The first runs parallel to the growth of the city's shoreline, and the second perpendicular. The brewery plants, collects, and distills *yuzu* to produce a liquor. The brewery building encompasses a distillery, a bar/restaurant, a shop, and an office. The water-ballast-powered funicular follows an existing drainage path of water on the hill and serves as a tool to both clear away old and construct new buildings. The architecture of each structure explores and negotiates the relationship between the built environment and the concept of emptiness.

Above: The brewery leverages the rhythm of the existing arcade and the vacancy after demolition. Right: The design reauthorizes the use of foundation debris left by the demolition of the original houses.

Left: The water-ballast-powered funicular. Top: The proposal lines the existing void, bracketing it against further development. Bottom: View from inside the bar/restaurant toward the patio.

Hearing Onomichi
Ruizhu Han

The intention of this project is to transform the experience of the town for both locals and visitors through the promotion of soundscapes: exhibitions, performances, and collaborative forms of music-making. Using sites in and around the city and hillside, the project "records" and "replays" the sounds of the city. Performance and sensorial recollections of the territory become key components of its identity and a means of its revitalization.

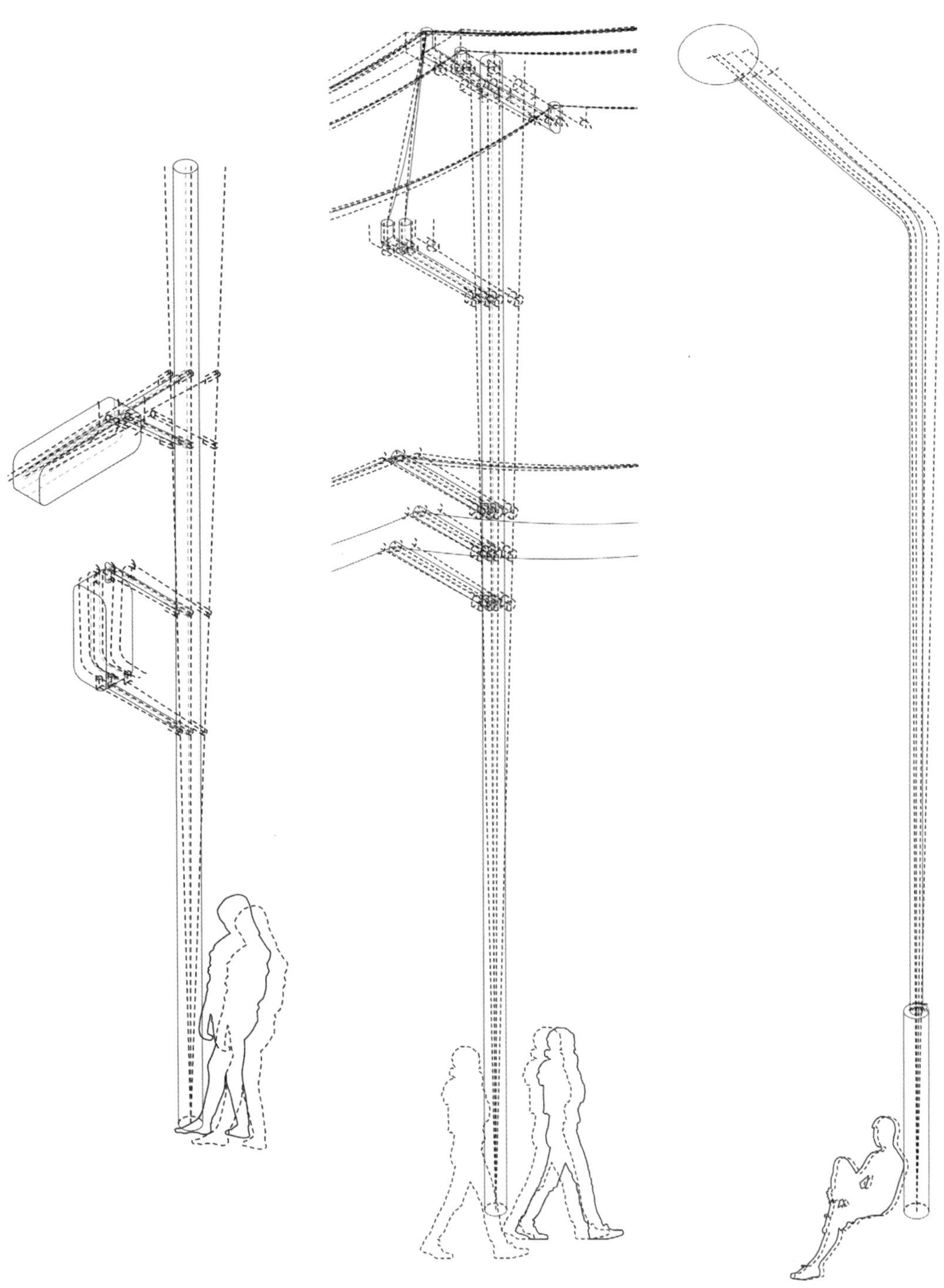

A variety of devices composes the project.

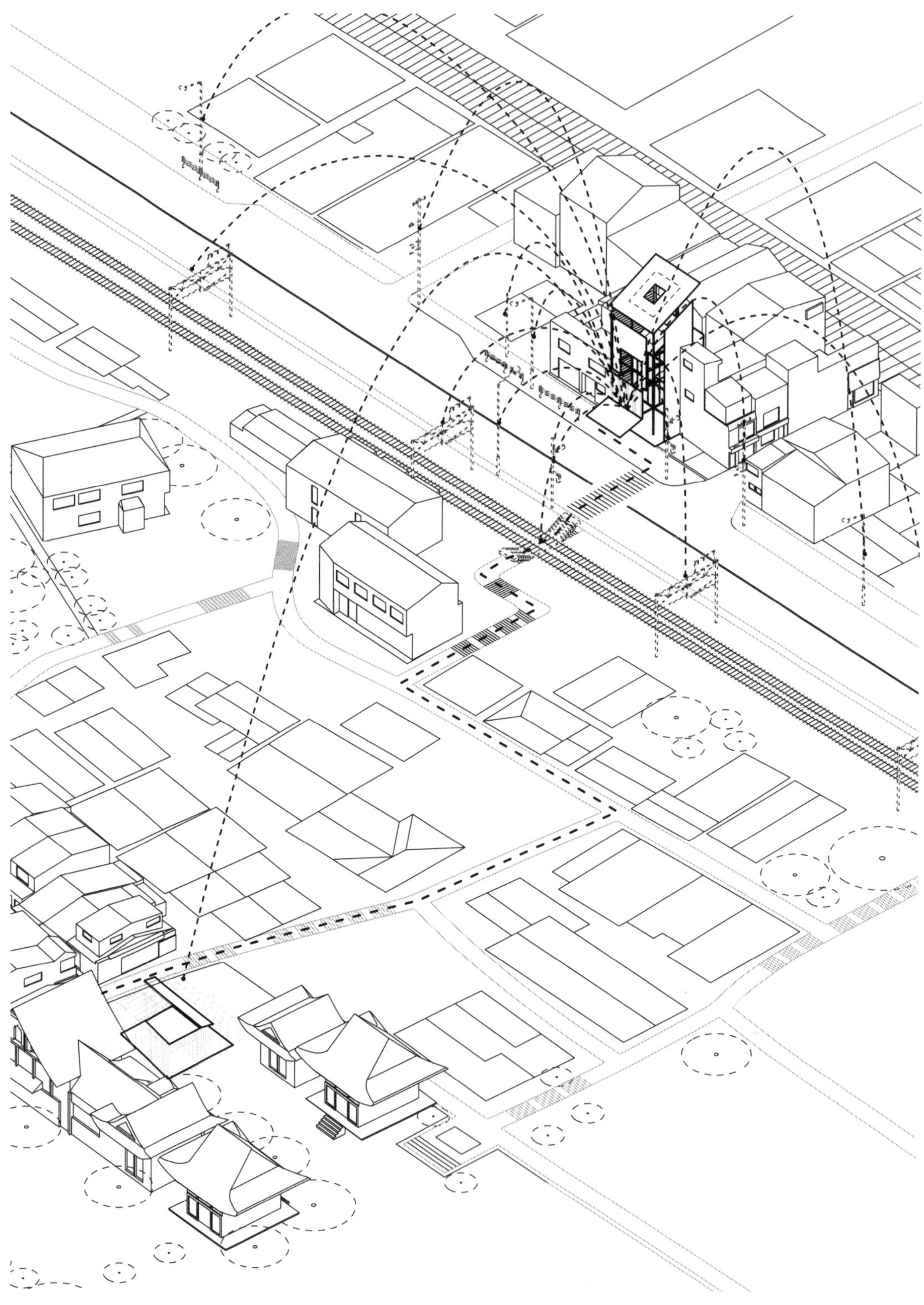

Hearing Onomichi is a system of collecting, replaying, and performing the sounds of the city at various locations by the seaside and on the hillside of the city.

Collective Domestic Choreography
Emily Hu

The aim of this project is to reinvent the everyday lives of people and reduce social isolation through the collectivization and choreography of domestic activities such as cooking and eating by reimagining and staging the scenes of everyday life. A large collective kitchen and fishing dock encourage socializing and reinforce the city's historic links to fishing. The architecture proposes different levels and degrees of porosity between the inside and the outside while recalibrating the relationship between the private and the public domains of the city.

A collective kitchen and fishing dock activate the seaside, fostering social interaction through cooking and eating together, and also reinforcing the city's old identity as a fishing port.

Fresh Onomichi
Yihan Liu

"Fresh Onomichi" consists of two parts: the "Super Arcade," a market and public space embedded in the Onomichi post office, and "Food Link," a small-scale cargo ropeway with two distribution centers—one located in the town and the other on the hillside—for transporting provisions to the residents of the hillside, including the elderly. The architecture of the "Super Arcade" explores the adaptive reuse of an existing building to rectify the current lack of easy access to a supermarket. Its modular timber construction is both flexible and sustainable: respectful of local traditions of construction, yet contemporary in its outlook. The "Food Link," on the other hand, provides a convenient way for mountain residents to purchase fresh produce.

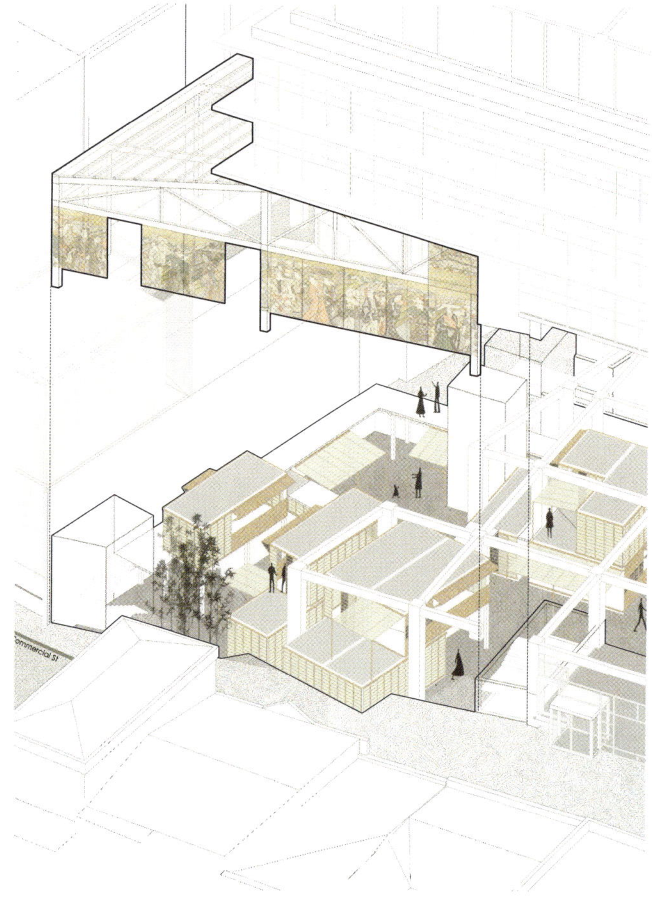

Super Arcade, a market created in the seaside downtown, comprises a modular construction system inserted in the existing main post office.

The new market is connected to the uphill neighborhood by Food Link, a cargo transportation system.

Gateway to Onomichi
Oonagh Davis

Onomichi is not only a port city but also a gateway to the Geiyo Archipelago in the Seto Inland Sea. A ferry terminal building, including a boatbuilding facility and a sailing school, will establish a stronger connection with the islands. The building will also contribute to the urban fabric of the city by its form and its location across from the railway station and bus terminal. Its timber structure explores the spatial characteristics and similarities between architecture and boatbuilding. The terminal's roof acts as a public space, offering views of the city, the waterfront, and the panorama beyond. The idea of an urban infrastructure is replicated at a much smaller scale on the hillside with a carpentry workshop and tool library for the community.

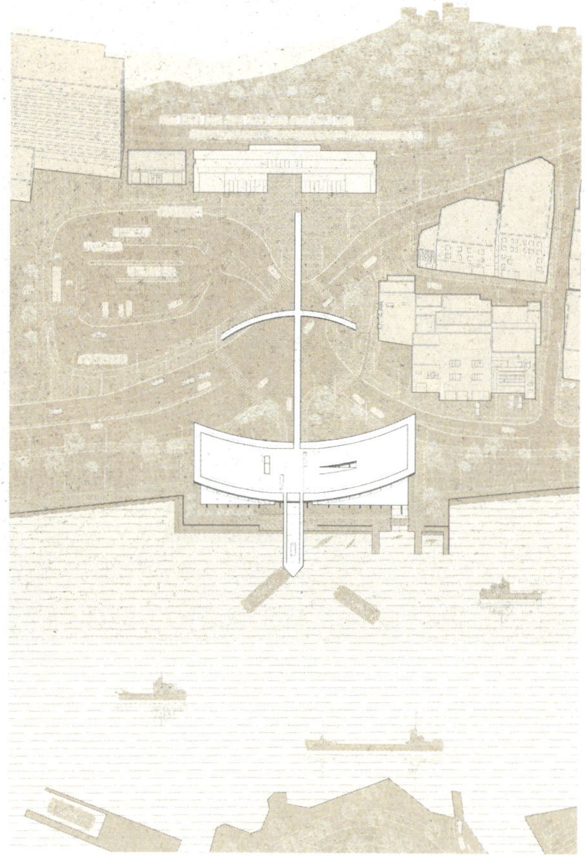

The project creates a trajectory connecting Mukaishima Island (bottom) to the new ferry terminal on the mainland, to the train station, and to the hillside (top).

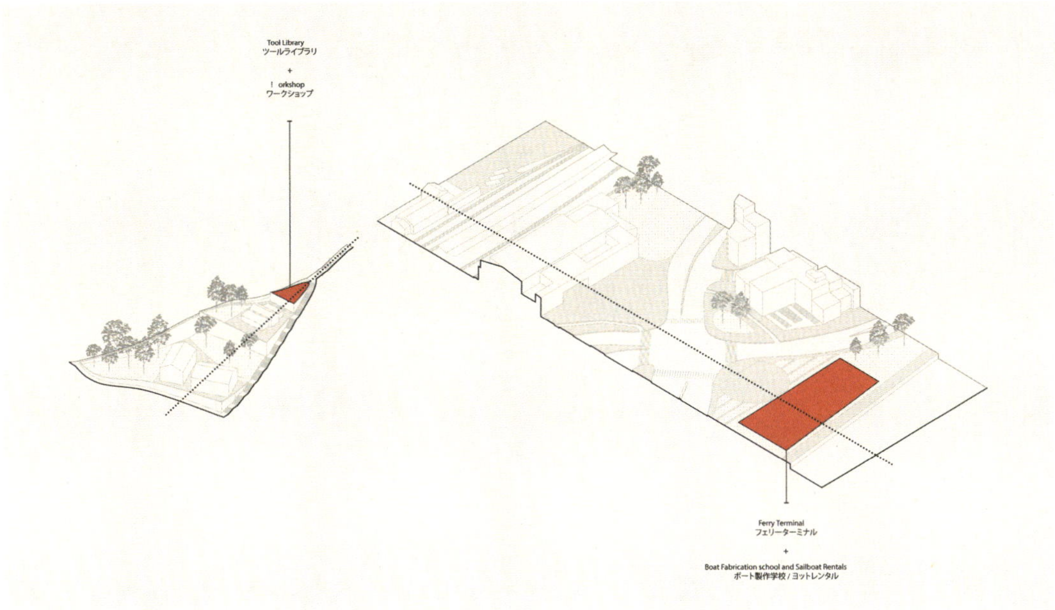

Top: Close-up view of the hybrid ferry terminal. The roof acts as a public space. Bottom: The project attempts to link the city's seaside (the ferry terminal) and the hillside (a carpentry workshop and tool library linked to the school in the ferry terminal).

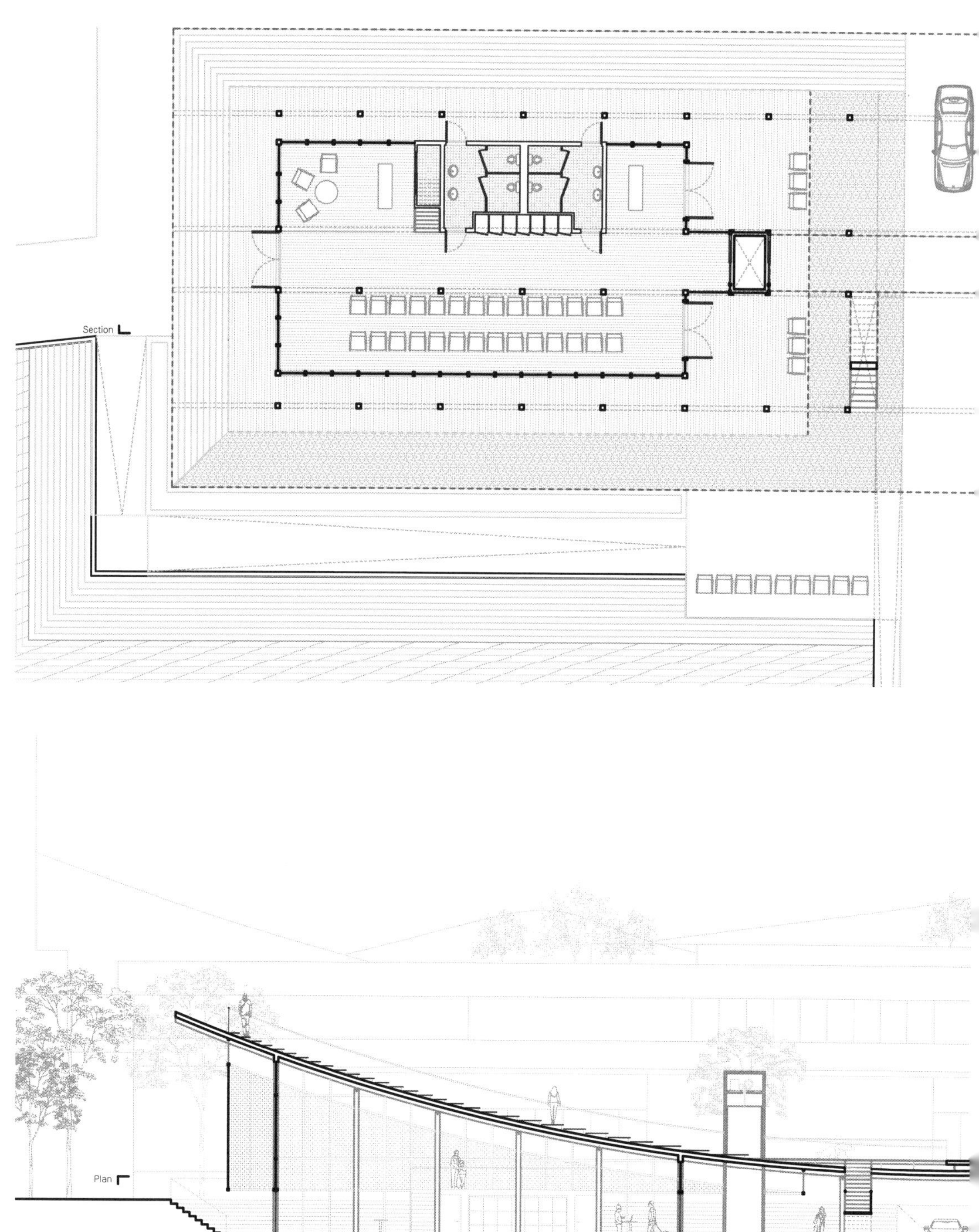

The ferry terminal comprises a variety of programs related to tourism and the local community.

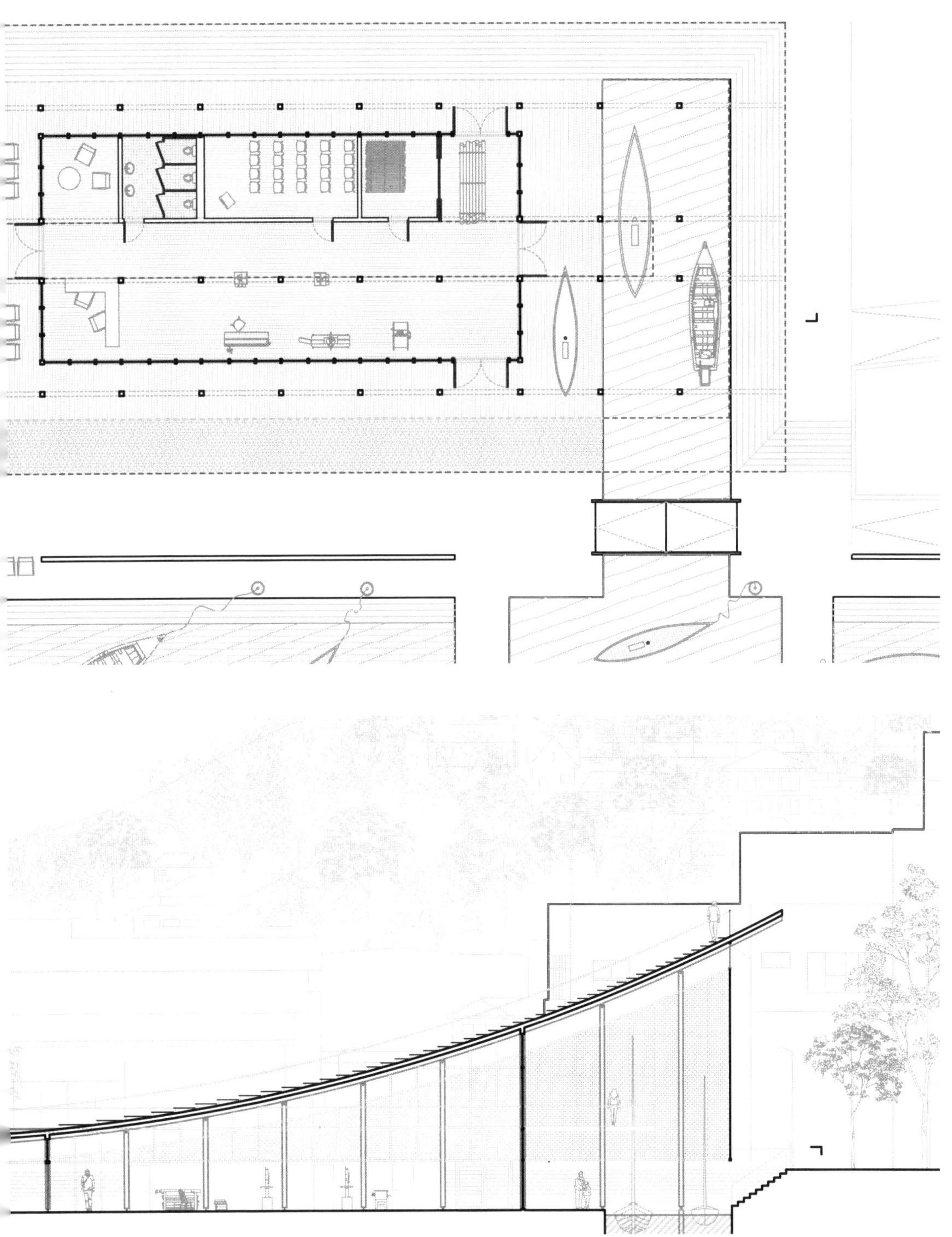

Yoro Shisetsu & Albergo Diffuso
Andreea Adam

At its core, this project explores the spatial and programmatic potentials of displacement. The elderly, many of whom live on the hillside, are both physically and socially isolated. This proposal conceptually transplants a fragment of the hillside to the seaside area of the city. The result is "Yoro Shisetsu," a sectional building/city that houses not only the elderly but also a series of facilities for youngsters, forming a joint care center where children and the elderly interact. The interstitial spaces, made up of terraces, landscapes, and gardens, enable and promote interaction between the users. The lower part of the project proposes a new urban public space and promenade for Onomichi.

A hillside proposal, "Albergo Diffuso," is based on the Italian concept of a hillside hotel with rooms in a series of buildings instead of only one. It reoccupies and transforms abandoned buildings and vacant lots to reimagine an alternative to conventional hotel accommodation that promotes local culture and authentic experiences. The process also reactivates the area.

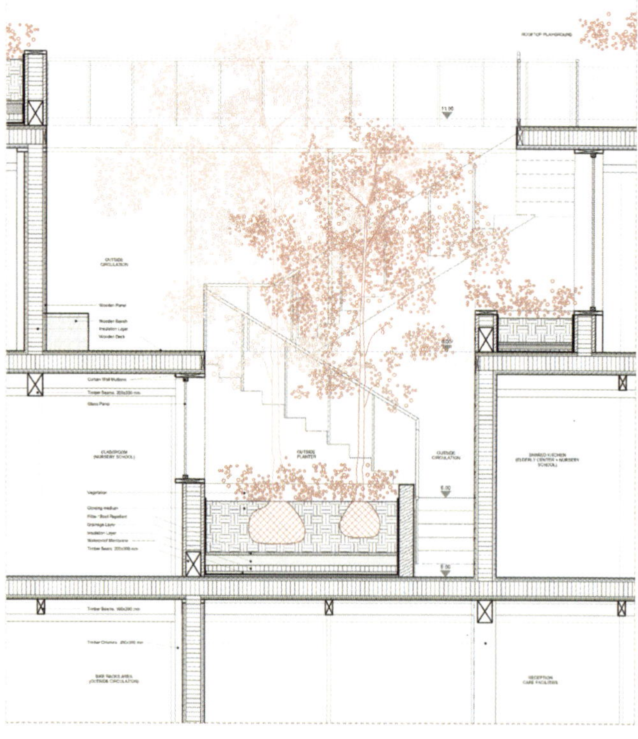

Yoro Shisetsu. Above: Section. Right: Aerial view. The cluster of buildings aims to promote the local culture and offer authentic experiences for tourists.

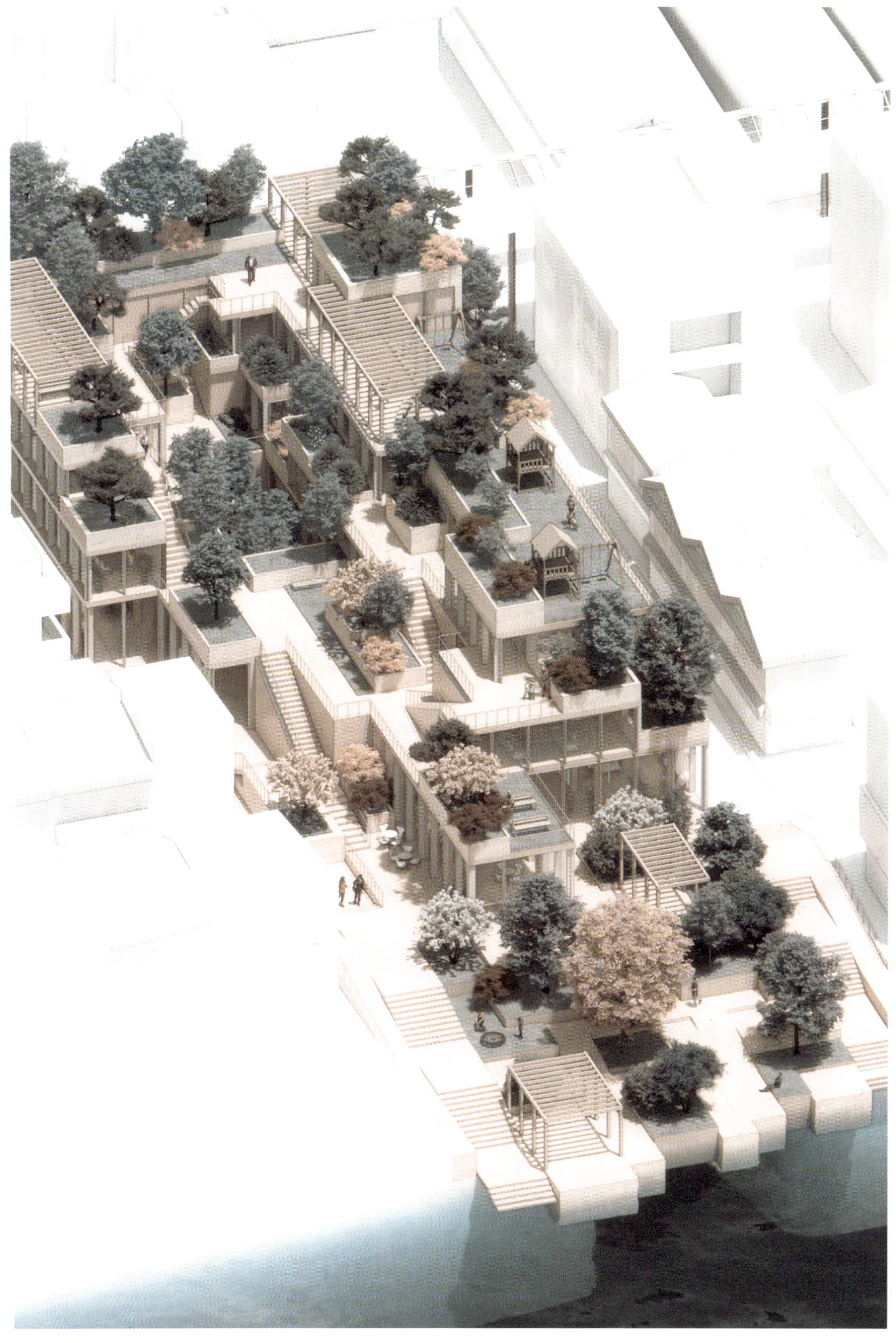

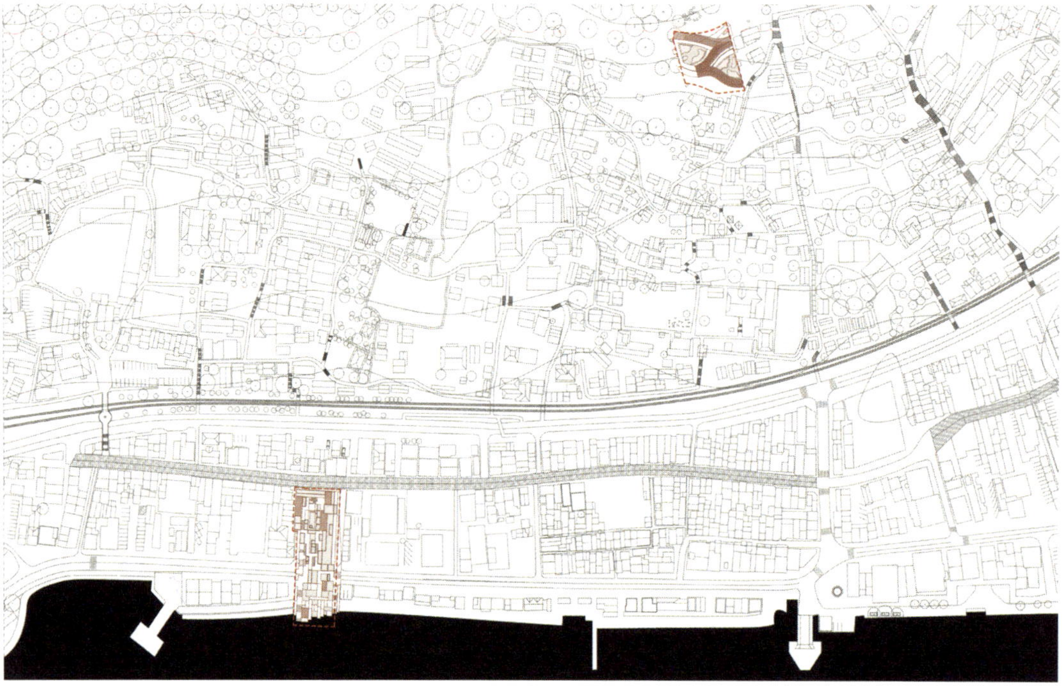

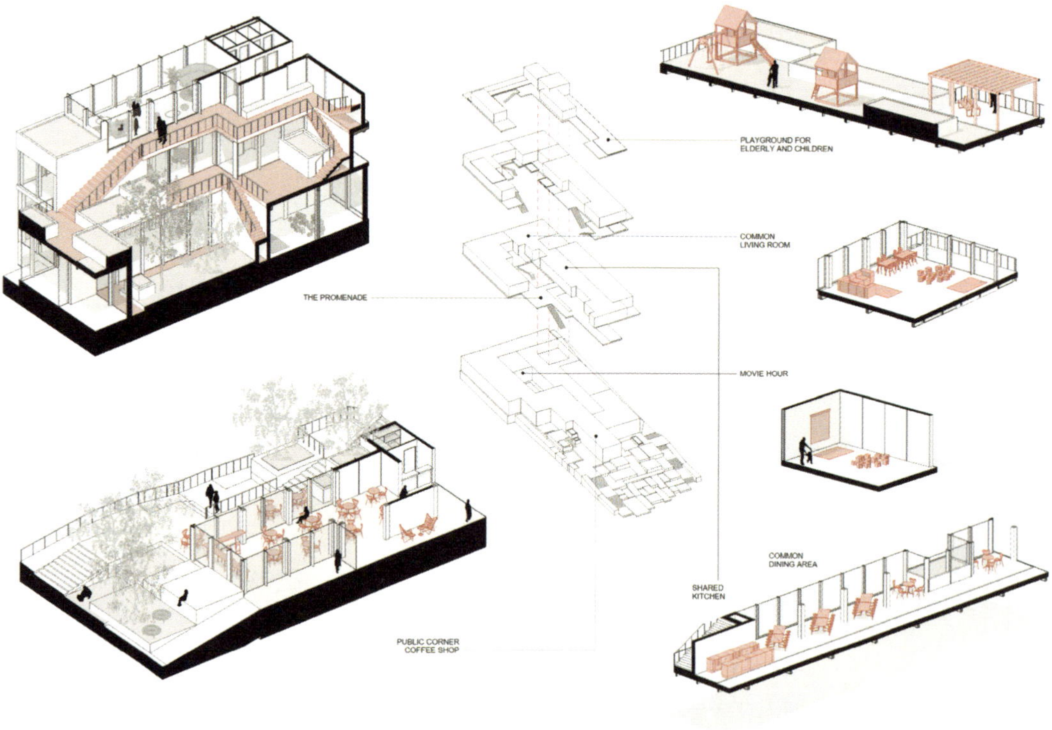

Top: The fragments of the project are oriented perpendicularly to the arcade and slowly fade into the water. Bottom: Detail of Yoro Shisetsu designed to meet the city's pressing issue—aging.

Top: Yoro Shisetsu comprises pixels to follow the hill pattern. Bottom: Albergo Diffuso both preserves and gives new life to the existing vacant buildings on the hillside.

Makerspace
Grace Cheng

The "Makerspace" targets local students, including those from the small local university on the outskirts of the town. It also speaks to Onomichi's strong interests in the arts. Operating as a hybrid workshop and community center, the facility enables students to visit for after-school programs, to make things, to study, and to socialize. Architecturally, the project aims to strengthen the links between the hillside and the seaside. Spatially, it recalls the Japanese concept of *ma* as a gap, a space in between two locations, to produce a new and yet familiar space for the community.

Above: The project aims to revitalize a densely built area in the city by inviting novel relationships among the existing and the new. Right: The complex is made by rotating similarly shaped frames.

Left: The courtyard connecting the volumes around it. Above: The roofs diminish the volumetric reading of the built structure.

Geography's Material and Intellectual Transformations

Conversation with Matthew Gandy

○ Mohsen Mostafavi: For the past few years, we've been working on a series of projects related to Japan and the future of urbanization. Some of this work is documented on the website Japan Story,[1] and we've also recently published a book called *Sharing Tokyo: Artifice and the Social World*.[2] One of the main tasks of this project is to help us understand and think beyond the spatial inequities that mark many privately owned large-scale projects in Tokyo.

What is your experience and reaction to the increasing "privatization" of contemporary metropolitan development? Do you see any lessons that can be learned from these projects?

● Matthew Gandy: It is very interesting that you are looking at these questions from a Japanese perspective. I think that one of the features of urban studies, broadly defined, is the sense of a shifting urban archetype as we look at the way Paris, Los Angeles, London, New York, Lagos, Mumbai, and a number of other cities have periodically served as leitmotifs or analytical entry points for the field. I am curious to know how your focus on Tokyo, and other metropolitan regions in Japan, alters the intellectual coordinates for thinking about the urban condition.

The question of privatization is fundamentally about the power of capital to shape urban space. We need to examine how perturbations in the circulation of global capital are reflected through periodicities in the transformation of cities. Distinctive historical periods include the rebuilding of Second Empire Paris under Baron Haussmann and mid-20th-century New York under Robert Moses. We encounter a series of specific conjunctions between power, capital, and the transformation of urban space. Within that framework, of course, there are constant tensions around the definition of the public interest or the public realm. There are repeated crises in relation to housing, public services, and other dimensions. And part of the struggle within the urban arena that Manuel Castells and others have described is how these collective dimensions of urban experience periodically come closer to some degree of democratic scrutiny or control. In other words, how is this process of urbanization to be shaped or guided? And who is this urban process actually for?

○ Just to stay with that for a second, some of the transformations that are happening or have happened recently in Japan are in part linked to the increasing implementation of neoliberal policies at the governmental level. Do you see, or are you aware of, any places where there have been slightly different approaches than those of neoliberal policies? I am thinking of the formation of

1 See japanstory.org.
2 Mohsen Mostafavi and Kayoko Ota, eds., *Sharing Tokyo: Artifice and the Social World* (New York: Actar, 2023).

new spatial conditions or spatial experiences that manage to avoid some of the negative consequences of these large-scale proposals that we see in major metropolitan capitals.

● Yes, I think if we look more broadly, we have this impetus toward neoliberal urban policy, including the privatization of public services, utilities, and things of that kind. But in certain circumstances, things can stop or even move in the opposite direction. One example that I find very interesting is in Berlin, where the privatized water utility, following a citywide referendum, was brought back under public control, and there are similar campaigns in other cities and municipalities. The important point here is to recognize that neoliberalism is not an inevitable singularity in relation to urban space. There are multiple pathways through urbanization and modernity. In this respect, I have been influenced by the work of the American philosopher Andrew Feenberg on alternative modernities, who incidentally also studied Japanese society.[3] By holding on to the idea that there are multiple pathways it becomes periodically possible to reconnect democratic deliberation with the urban process.

○ Today, Japan seems to exemplify the concept of a degrowth society. Cities like Tokyo, because of their size and their enormous population, at least for the time being, seem to be more immune to the consequences of depopulation. They have so many people coming in that you don't notice that they are depopulating. But Japan is not the only country facing the combination of an increasing elderly population together with a low birth rate, a situation that is exacerbated by Japan's immigration policies. The impact of these forces is much more evident in rural locations, away from the main metropolitan centers like Tokyo and Osaka, with growing numbers of abandoned houses and schools. How common are these demographic changes in other parts of the world and what is being done to address the issue?

● I think this theme of demographic decline and urban shrinkage is extremely interesting and presents different possibilities in terms of how to respond, especially in the context of increasingly reactionary political agendas in relation to migration and multiculturalism. In Germany, for example, some municipalities have explicitly stated that they are "safe havens" and will welcome refugees. And there are sometimes very interesting debates in these smaller towns about the idea that families and children will return to these communities so that old people can hear the sound of children's laughter and so on. Communities can

3 See, for example, Andrew Feenberg, *Alternative Modernity: The Technical Turn in Philosophy and Social Theory* (Berkeley, CA: University of California Press, 1995).

suddenly become full of life. I think this is a very important challenge to reactionary discourses about refugees and migration. Interestingly, the German urban sociologist Hartmut Häußermann raised these points some years ago in terms of regarding migration as a potential solution to the demographic decline of shrinking cities.

○ As a geographer, how much do you have to be conscious of the way in which productive ideas simultaneously can have the potential to spark opposite reactions in other parts of society? For example, the welcoming of migration might go hand in hand with the rise of certain demonstrations of racism or that kind of inflammatory response. I'm wondering whether the promotion of good ideas or positive, productive ideas must at some point anticipate its own opposite. And whether that's something that's thought about in contemporary social thought or geography?

● As academics we have responsibilities to do good research but also to be educators, to respond to and engage with important debates that are going on. Of course, there has been this drift toward not just xenophobic politics but also toward anti-metropolitan, anti-science, and anti-expertise sentiments. The status of the academic has never been more precarious than in recent years. But I think that we have to withstand these kinds of pressures, and specifically in relation to the migration debate we need to challenge populist or authoritarian political movements that try to blame marginal or vulnerable groups in society for problems that are structural in origin, such as increased levels of economic precarity and social inequality. I think there is a responsibility across not just the social sciences but also the humanities and other disciplines to come forward with very carefully reasoned counterviews and not to allow a false consensus to emerge.

○ At Harvard, we have devoted a part of our research to studying the city of Onomichi, a port city in the western part of the country with a long tradition of shipbuilding. Now, with those industries in decline, the city needs to find new ways to revive itself as a viable home for its decreasing population. As architects and urbanists, some of our proposals involve the greater provision of infrastructure and services for the community, including the elderly and the young. Enhancing the quality of life in the city of Onomichi seems to be the only way to not only support the local population but also to stop or reduce migration to larger cities that offer greater opportunities. This approach has the potential to make the city more attractive to internal migration as well as local tourism.

The Japanese Marxist philosopher Kohei Saito, in his book *Marx in the Anthropocene*, makes the argument for what he calls degrowth communism.[4] What are your thoughts about the topic of degrowth and Saito's position?

● I'm very glad you mentioned Saito's work because I think that this is really making a major impact across geography, sociology, and other disciplines with certain parallels to the work of Andreas Malm. Within the social sciences and the humanities, I think there has been an element of impatience about not coming forward with more radical and conceptually innovative policy-oriented positions in relation to the global environmental crisis. What's especially fascinating about Saito's work is that he has gone back to Marx's original notebooks, unpublished works, and other archival sources to refresh our understanding of Marx's writing about the environment and his original articulation of "metabolic rift" in relation to capitalist agriculture, illuminating Marx's wider concerns with deforestation, intensive farming methods, cruelty to animals, and so on. Saito provides a broader perspective of Marx's original sense of a fundamental contradiction between capital and the biosphere by introducing a more broad-based set of very interesting conceptual ideas concerning what he terms "metabolic shift." The core idea is that capitalism constantly seeks to delay or displace any constraints through measures such as nuclear-powered desalination plants or other types of technological fixes. Saito's interpretation connects with some of the existing work in geography by Erik Swyngedouw and others in relation to the "socio-ecological fix." Capital has a chameleon-like ability to absorb critique and alter its configurations without ever really addressing fundamental contradictions. I think what is important for Saito, Foster, and other scholars is the sense that these contradictions cannot be avoided forever. Indeed, these contradictions are much closer now in terms of global health threats, climatic disruption, and so on. The key challenges are now much more pressing in terms of what alternatives exist to an ever-expanding capitalist global system and whether we can address these ecological contradictions. Many environmentalists and eco-modernists suggest that this historical trajectory can be altered by a variety of market mechanisms and technological innovations.
In contrast, Saito and others are saying that this clearly will not work. We need something much more radical. This is why the whole degrowth agenda is so interesting—it has multiple implications not just for the economy but also for the structuring of everyday life. The implications might be that we work fewer hours in the week and use that extra time doing other things, such as tending allotments or connecting with people. In addition to the nature of work there are spatial implications,

too. Instead of urban space conceived as an arena for hyper-consumerism, we can focus on other, more life-affirming aspects. There are clearly spatial as well as political implications to the kind of arguments that Saito is making. I think it is an exciting moment in terms of the reinvigoration of some of the original works of Marx and the development of radical ecological critique.

○ This relates very much to the town of Onomichi. One of its key physical characteristics is how the main part of the town is next to a port, built on reclaimed land, and is juxtaposed with the more "natural" setting of a hillside dotted with houses and temples. Many of the houses become abandoned when their owners pass away. Others have become ruins with nature taking over the site.

In your own work, in particular the book *Natura Urbana: Ecological Constellations in Urban Space*, you speak of "urban nature as a multilayered material and symbolic entity."[5] What do you see as the connections between your interests in urban ecology and the broader discussions of the opportunities offered by degrowth?

● Words such as "nature" or "ecology" are incredibly complex from the outset, and one of the things that I'm interested in is a kind of a double history of nature. On the one hand, there are a series of material transformations, including the return of nature to abandoned spaces and things of that kind. On the other hand, there is a changing historical dynamic in terms of intellectual thought in relation to ecology and nature. For me, a key analytical challenge is to try to elucidate the connections between material transformations and intellectual transformations. This is what I mean by a double history. One particular challenge I faced in writing my book is how to handle a vast and growing literature in relation to urban ecology and urban nature. Over the last 20 years there has been an explosion of ideas and literature on the environmental dimensions to cities and urbanization.

In order to make sense of the changing field I have developed a kind of working typology of four main perspectives in the literature. The first of these is what I call "systems-based approaches," which are in many ways the dominant perspective in relation to architecture, planning, engineering, design, and other professional fields. In my book I also emphasize three other important strands: observational paradigms linked to natural history, including links to urban botany, urban ornithology, and a variety of direct encounters with nature in

4 Kohei Saito, *Marx in the Anthropocene: Towards the Idea of Degrowth Communism* (Cambridge: Cambridge University Press, 2023).

5 Matthew Gandy, *Natura Urbana: Ecological Constellations in Urban Space* (Cambridge: MIT Press, 2022).

cities; the neo-Marxian-inspired urban political ecology that emphasizes contested dimensions to capitalist urbanization; and the more recent rise of interest in multispecies urbanism drawing on insights from multispecies ethnographies, the ecological pluriverse, and attempts to think through different ways of living with nonhuman others. What is especially interesting to me is the possibility of articulating some kind of conceptual synthesis between these different strands that can help us take these arguments forward so that if we're interested in the multispecies city we can extend ethical questions beyond, for example, the feeding of garden birds to thinking about agro-capitalism and the production of food, which is where urban political ecology can be very helpful in terms of highlighting the circulatory dynamics of capital and the significance of extractive frontiers. In thinking about these four different perspectives, I remain uncertain whether the systems-based approach can be further elaborated or whether we need a complete break with that particular way of conceptualizing urban space. Just recently, however, I went to a very interesting workshop in Brussels organized by LAB [Louvain research institute for landscape, architecture, and the built environment] where possibilities for elaborating on systems-based models were widely discussed. A particular focus was whether the so-called Brussels school of urban ecology, associated with the ideas of the ecologist Paul Duvigneaud, might be extended through a variety of advanced modeling techniques drawing on new sources of quantitative data. A key dilemma remains, however, in terms of the conceptual limitations of systems-based understandings of capitalist urbanization as a series of material flows rather than a historical process.

○ Architects and urbanists design buildings and cities, but we are very conscious of the interrelationships between the physical and social worlds from a multiplicity of perspectives. In this context, we have tried to understand and incorporate into our work lessons from the Japanese philosopher Tetsuro Watsuji and his development of the Japanese concept of Fudo, or milieu, and the articulation of the concept of Umwelt, the environment understood from multiple perspectives, human and nonhuman, from Jakob von Uexküll.

In addition to your own work, others, including the British geographer Sarah Whatmore, have been interested in a broader understanding of "living cities" as what she has called the "living fabric of associations." How might this expanded and shifting articulation of social relations, including multispecies relations, reframe our future speculations about urbanization?

● Let me briefly respond to this interesting influence of the Japanese philosopher Tetsuro Watsuji because it seems that the *milieu* idea emerges from the French geographer Augustin Berque's attempt to bring some of Watsuji's ideas to European audiences. We can see connections here with a certain kind of European tradition of phenomenology. This cross-fertilization of ideas between Japan and Europe is interesting. So perhaps the first point to make is that notions of phenomenology have become more influential across a range of fields, and they've been linked in certain ways with the neo-vitalist or new materialist impulse, which has been quite significant within geography, sociology, and other disciplines. Now what really interests me, because by and large I take a skeptical stance toward new materialist approaches, are these unresolved questions concerning the distinctiveness of human historical agency in relation to this radically expanded conception of agency and subjects. I think this is a very important intellectual focal point for these discussions about the contours of nonhuman agency within urban space. Consider, for example, recent contributions by the German sociologist Thomas Lemke or the Cambridge-based geographer Maan Barua. There is a very interesting discussion going on about the implications of an expanded philosophical framework that moves beyond the agency of the individual or collective human subject. And within my own discipline of geography, of course, the work of people such as Sarah Whatmore has made an important early contribution to these debates. A stimulus to critical reflection has been the return of nature to cities—consider, for example, foxes in London, coyotes in North American cities, and leopards in and around Indian cities. These emerging socio-ecological relations present all kinds of interesting questions and debates. An unresolved tension in the post-humanist impulse is how to handle ethical relations with nonhuman others within the terrain of public health and epidemiology. What are we to do if there is a perceived public health threat over the presence of rats in cities? In Paris, for instance, this has provoked extensive and increasingly polarized public debate. There is now an interesting debate about the possibility to move away from the use of culls or poisoned bait to get rid of unwanted nonhuman others within cities and turn instead to more ethical, humane, and technologically sophisticated alternatives such as the use of contraception for animals.

A related issue is that when we think about urban epidemiology and threats of disease, exacerbated by climate change, inadequate infrastructure, poverty, and other factors, and in particular aspects of aquatic ecologies and flood control within cities, we're going to have to confront the increased threat of insect-vectors for disease such as mosquitoes. This is going to pose significant implications for urban design and urban planning. One of the terms that I find quite useful to work with is that of an affirmative biopolitical paradigm. In other words, the sense that, from a philosophical position, an insistence on "non-intervention" is very difficult to sustain and that we are faced with a series of very real dilemmas in relation to how, and under what circumstances, we do intervene in—or at least try to steer—biophysical or ecological processes, which of course extends to urban epidemiological questions. This notion of an affirmative biopolitical paradigm could in certain respects also be applied to plants and landscape design. There are some very interesting approaches to landscape design which allow unexpected or spontaneous floras to flourish in certain parts of urban space, a development that lies in stark contrast to the control of ecological processes elsewhere. This introduces a notion of temporality into architecture and landscape design because sometimes there is a public sentiment that certain sites should be protected and left alone, assuming that a flower-rich interstitial space such as a wasteland or railway embankment will simply remain the same. But this doesn't happen in relation to void spaces since a space that is left alone will be transformed by its own dynamics. Many of these "urban meadows" will become urban woodlands over time which is a very different kind of ecological space. To have an enriched public discourse about these questions, I think it is necessary to move beyond the sense of non-intervention, toward a more critically engaged discussion about how to shape urban nature or urban ecological processes.

○ I'd like to ask you if you could somehow relate these ideas to the work of Raymond Williams. In your own work, the *Natura Urbana* for example, this mixing of nature and city, this idea that there is a hybrid moment when a landscape is inseparable from the artifice of the city, seems far away from Williams's book *The Country and the City.*[6] Even though he was at that time articulating these relationalities, the difference between the country and the city was still very distinct. Today this distinctness is disappearing perhaps. But when you visit a town like Onomichi or any small town, these differences between the metropolitan capitals and the idea of the market town, industrial small towns, regional cities, or regional towns remain.

What do you remember of Raymond Williams or what remains as part of his lineage today for people like yourself?

● Strangely enough, in my university lectures this term I have been referring directly to Raymond Williams's book *The Country and the City,* dating from 1973, which I think is in many ways just as interesting as when it was first published. When we think about the work of Williams there are of course many elements, but I would like to briefly mention two ideas that are very important. One is his classic intervention in terms of the etymology of the word "nature," reminding us that it is one of the most complex words in the English language. I think that holding on to this notion of etymological complexity is very important across the whole field of environmental discourse. We should always be thinking quite carefully about the polyvalent or shifting meaning of words and their relationship to ideological constructs such as national identity. The other idea I would like to mention is his zonal conception of interrelated landscapes. We find, for example, that the landscaped grounds of stately homes are set within the rationalized landscapes of agricultural enclosure that are in turn connected to the brutality of more distant plantation landscape under European colonialism. This multi-scalar conception of zonal landscapes is still very relevant when we consider the production of designed spaces in cities. One example is the High Line in Manhattan that has been widely praised as a kind of urban oasis but is actually more like the eye of the storm within accelerating gentrification pressures in Chelsea and adjacent Manhattan neighborhoods, that are in turn linked to global economic dynamics. A multi-scalar perspective à la Williams is very helpful in terms of articulating a critical design discourse in urban space.

○ You have been incredibly generous in your answers by situating your responses within the context of current scholarship. You've mentioned a variety of authors and their publications and their contributions. But in closing, it would be wonderful if you could speak a little bit about where geography is going today, and what are some of the key emergent directions or thoughts that you feel will be important pathways toward the future questions of urbanization.

● Yes. Interesting question. It's strange because if you're inside a discipline and you're immersed in this almost endless stream of discussion it is sometimes hard to pick the key things out from the noise in terms of how a discipline is shaping or evolving. I have always read very widely beyond the narrow confines of geography. I mentioned Kohei Saito and Andreas Malm, who incidentally is a human geographer based in Sweden. I was excited, by the way, to see that one of his books has recently been made into a very impressive independent film, *How to Blow Up a Pipeline.*[7] It is unusual, I would say, for an academic work to be made into a critically acclaimed and commercially successful film.

6 Raymond Williams, *The Country and the City* (London: Chatto & Windus, 1973).
7 *How to Blow Up a Pipeline* (Dir.: Daniel Goldhaber, 2023).

In terms of influences or emerging influences, I would have to pick out the cultural theorist Sianne Ngai, based at the University of Chicago. What I find fascinating about her work, which connects incidentally to the critical neo-Marxian oeuvre of Raymond Williams, Fredric Jameson, and other scholars, is a sense that many of the conceptual terms or categories that we are using are highly anachronistic. We are working with an 18th- or 19th-century conceptual vocabulary to deal with fundamentally new challenges in the 21st century. Equally, in a similar fashion to Saito, I think Ngai is very particular about holding on to the very idea of critique. She has recently emphasized the need for a "post-post-critical" approach as part of a commitment to serious critical scholarship.

○ It's interesting that you mentioned Ngai. We were recently talking about some of these aesthetic categories, for example in the context of Japan, and in particular—I use this very carefully—the notion of cuteness. In the context of certain cultures, there are many moments when things are appreciated specifically through the perspective of the aesthetics of cuteness.

What do you think about this question of aesthetic categories and their relevance to how we judge things and make decisions? How is that changing?

● Ngai has developed a novel conceptual lexicon, introducing the terms "zany," "cute," and "interesting," as part of a wider challenge to the persistence of somewhat anachronistic aesthetic categories such as "beauty" and the "sublime."[8] In some of my recent work, in collaboration with my colleague Maroš Krivý, based at the Estonian Academy of Arts, I have been reflecting on the idea of the zany à la Ngai in relation to the performativity of work within the neoliberal academy.[9] It is interesting to consider, particularly in relation to architecture and landscape design, how intellectual labor has changed. I would bring in here critical legal scholars such as Zoe Adams who have explored the extent of unpaid overtime within fields of creative knowledge production.[10] This is in addition to the various kinds of affective labor that are required within many professional fields, such as the specific intellectual milieu of the architectural or design studio. There are clear parallels here with what the economist Claudia Goldin refers to as "greedy jobs" that demand long hours and exacerbate existing inequalities in the workforce and wider society.

8 Sianne Ngai, *Our Aesthetic Categories: Zany, Cute, Interesting* (Cambridge, MA: Harvard University Press, 2012).
9 See Maroš Krivý and Matthew Gandy, "Zany Beetroot: Architecture, Autopoiesis, and the Spatial Formations of Late Capital," *Environment and Planning: Society and Space* (in press).
10 Zoe Adams, "Invisible Labour: Legal Dimensions of Invisibilization," *Journal of Law and Society* 49 (2) (2022): 385–405.

○ Matthew, thank you so much. It has been wonderful to hear you talk about all these different topics.

Postscript

Kayoko Ota

A new layer of architectural creations has emerged in Japan during the last two decades. Found in regional cities and provinces, these works demonstrate a new kind of strength, achieved by tackling degrowth and depopulation, the increasingly pressing social challenges of our time.

The vigor comes from an ability to encourage alternative ways of living and social interaction, encompassing a larger and longer framework for the urban fabric or the community than is usual for just a building. This innovative approach suggests a new value in architecture that will be increasingly important to acquire and develop in the changed society, a value marked by a shift away from the aesthetic or philosophical priorities of the past.

This architectural power is discreet. The work may not make outstanding gestures in terms of form; it exerts its power in a more subtle manner, through a careful redefinition of planning in terms of program, design process, and space as a medium for navigating people's behaviors. It's an architecture in an active voice without flamboyance.

Outside the Market Regime

Architects with small- to medium-sized practices get few opportunities to work in large cities, where it has become standard practice to apply a specific set of approaches to planning and design. As the neoliberal doctrine demands, the priority is on producing more marketable floor area to boost the economy.

But the situation is different in regional cities and provinces. They are in desperate need of a means of revitalization, not commodification. The agenda of programming new buildings is more about enhancing communities, promoting inclusiveness, and showing openness to visitors and immigrants so that the city or region can survive. It's critical for the declining community to foster a high quality of life through enhanced social interaction, which would improve the circumstances for raising children, attract more visitors and immigrants, and increase population and economic activities. Some architects are beginning to take advantage of this situation, largely freed from the undesirable forces of the market economy.

Another advantage is that the expectations for the profession are rising in a shrinking condition. While there persisted for a long time a skepticism toward architects as difficult yet inevitable guest players, today they are relied upon for their expertise of thinking in space and the increased ability to collaborate with the client and users. Outside the market regime, architects can find more flexibility to explore architecture in an unconventional way due to the desperateness of the social condition.

As the background for this new approach, I should note that architects, especially those in the young generation, are more and more engaged in the non-metropolitan areas with a new professional ethics, largely due to the significant impact of the 2011 Great East Japan (Tohoku) earthquake and tsunami. Those in their 30s and 40s today have never experienced economic growth. For all their lives they have seen various communities suffer from a declining economy and natural disasters. Now they aspire to bring sober solutions to the immediate issues rather than delineate the distant future as auteurs-philosophers like Kazuo Shinohara and Arata Isozaki.

A New Landscape

Hence, new types of architecture are emerging. With the works of Kumiko Inui and Jun Aoki, we clearly see the fruit of the changing condition for architects in regional cities and provinces. Their role is expanding from a conventional scope of work, which in general does not begin until after the basic planning phase. In designing a public building, Inui was granted the authority to revert from the design phase back to the planning phase in order to achieve conceptual integrity, while Aoki was allowed to experiment on programs with future users from the early conception stage. Both pushed the limit of architecture to create such common ground, an approach that continues to be favored by the public.

The positive change in architects' working conditions and relationships with clients and users is linked to the proliferation of the participatory design process, which in Japan was pioneered by the community designer Ryo Yamazaki and his firm studio-L. Extending architects' obligations while diversifying design inputs for them, the community designers empower both building users and architects while revitalizing regions across the country.

Takahito Ito and Miho Tominaga, for example, acquire mastery by surrendering to what's outside their own knowledge, using their thorough research to fuel creativity. Jo Nagasaka has opened up the possibility of alternative development through his strategic thinking, which always involves the neighbors and the community around a project site and encompasses a longer time span. His strength subtly yet steadily infiltrates people's minds and affects the landscape of the neighborhood.

Both Yutaro Muaji and Koki Akiyoshi chose to confront the social challenge of housing by inventing a system of relinking existing resources (abandoned apartments) or industries (forestry) to the expanded options of housing. Both set up a socially oriented venture as young entrepreneurs. In some way, they resonate with the Metabolist group around 1960 who presented a new visionary plan for rebuilding cities on tabula rasa. But the young visionaries today are committed to tackling real-world problems.

A new vigor is emerging in regional cities and provinces. As Toyo Ito proposes in his essay, that is the fertile ground for cultivating architectural creativity. The harvest will offer a different sort of wealth than in the past, one that helps sustain and enrich life under the no-growth condition.

KOKI AKIYOSHI is an architect and the CEO of VUILD, founded in 2017 with the goal of democratizing architecture. Calling himself a "meta architect," he is extending a network of creative platforms across Japan whereby anyone can fabricate their own furniture and building designs. By integrating forest resources and digital fabrication technology, he covers a wide range of design from object to social revitalization.

JUN AOKI is an architect and a partner in the architecture firm AS. Acclaimed for his Louis Vuitton flagship stores design, Aoki has also demonstrated ingenuity in works ranging from art installation to housing to museums to renovation for social revitalization. Since 2019 he has been the director of the Kyoto City Kyocera Museum of Art, which he renovated with Tetsuo Nishizawa.

MATTHEW GANDY is a geographer and urbanist. He is Professor of Cultural and Historical Geography at the University of Cambridge. He has been recognized for his scholarship in areas such as the depiction of nature in the visual arts, infrastructure, water, and urban metabolism and biodiversity. His most recent book is *Natura Urbana: Ecological Constellations in Urban Space* (2022).

KENTA HASEGAWA is a photographer. He earned recognition among architects of the younger generation in Japan, including Jo Nagasaka and Yutaro Muraji, for his new approach to everyday urban life and generic spaces like that of the Narita Airport Terminal 3. He documented the relationship of the urban space and nature for *Sharing Tokyo: Artifice and the Social World.*

KUMIKO INUI is an architect and the principal of Inui Architects. She has worked on large-scale public buildings in various parts of Japan that are designed to nurture the commons. Her design approach, based on thorough research and communication with the users of her projects—large and small, public and private—has garnered acclaim for expanding the role of architectural design.

TAKAHITO ITO is an architect and the principal of AMP/PAM, a design firm focused on creating community hubs in and around Tokyo by means of renovation. His guiding design principle is founded on maintaining the existing urban elements of any scale—from street to urban district to landscape—as socially shared assets. Until 2020, he was a partner in the firm tomito architecture.

TOYO ITO is an architect and the principal of Toyo Ito & Associates, Architects. Since setting up his practice in 1971, Ito has been a pioneer on the architectural front in Japan, both as a designer and as a thinker. He has also been actively engaged in social revitalization in Japan through architecture, steering the Home-for-All and Kumamoto Artpolis programs.

MOHSEN MOSTAFAVI is the Alexander and Victoria Wiley Professor of Design and a Harvard University Distinguished Service Professor. He leads the Japan Research Initiative at the Harvard Graduate School of Design. His publications and collaborations include *Ethics of the Urban: The City and the Spaces of the Political* (2017) and *Sharing Tokyo: Artifice and the Social World* (2023).

YUTARO MURAJI is an architect and the founding principal of CHAr (Commons for Habitat and Architecture). During his time in a PhD program, he organized workshops for regenerating old wooden apartments (*mokuchin*) in Tokyo. The initiative grew into a social venture for regenerating challenged housing resources and enhancing social connectivity. In 2018 he was selected as a Social Innovator by the Nippon Foundation.

JO NAGASAKA is an architect and the principal of Schemata Architects. Whether designing furniture or architecture or engaged in area regeneration, he finds value in the ordinary in the existing context with a particular focus on materiality. For Nagasaka, renovation is a new genre of design that can strategically enhance social revitalization. His work sites are expanding in Japan and abroad.

KAYOKO OTA is an architectural curator and editor. Before joining the Japan Research Initiative at the Harvard University Graduate School of Design, she curated a series of the CCA c/o Tokyo programs for the Canadian Centre for Architecture and was commissioner of the Japan Pavilion at the 2014 Venice Architecture Biennale. Her editorial work includes *Project Japan: Metabolism Talks...* (2011).

MIHO TOMINAGA is an architect and partner in tomito architecture, which she set up with Takahito Ito in 2014. Her design work begins with observing and representing the daily life around a site with her own speculative fantastical hand drawings, which enhances communication. She makes it a principle to create places for diverse users to be, which are woven into the land's narratives.

RYO YAMAZAKI is a community designer and the CEO of studio-L. Since launching in 2005, the firm has raised public awareness of the effective role of community design in Japan and helped local administration bodies integrate residents' participation in the process of designing public buildings and places. Studio-L also makes master plans, in consultation with residents, and helps communities create their own shared activities.

We wish to express our cordial appreciation and gratitude to the following people and organizations, each of whom generously supported our research and this publication:

Noriko Deno
Whana Hong
Ami Ishihara
Office for Kumamoto Artpolis, Kumamoto Prefectural Government
Natsuko Matsui
Chihiro Nakashima
Masami Nakata
Yuma Ota
Kanako Sekimori
Masako Toyota, Onomichi Akiya Saisei Project
Maya Utsunomiya
Ryuichiro Wada, Onomichi City Office
Zhiyan Wang
Satoko Yokoyama

Special thanks to the Takenaka Corporation and its honorary chairman, Mr. Toichi Takenaka, for their generous support of the Japan Research Initiative at the Harvard University Graduate School of Design.
—Mohsen Mostafavi and Kayoko Ota

Photographs:

© Iwan Baan: 18–19, 24–25
© Osamu Murai, Courtesy of Kumi Murai: 22
© Takumi Ota: 26–27, 174–177, 180–181 (center), 186–187
© Daici Ano: 40–41, 45, 49–51, 55–57, 80–82, 84–85
© Inui Architects: 44
© Shinkenchiku-sha: 52–53, 69, 72–73, 76–77, 98–99
© The Asahi Shimbun Company: 60
© Yoshihiko Takeuchi: 62, 78–79
© Shoichi Ishimaru: 68, Courtesy of the Office of Kumamoto Artpolis
© AS: 70–71
© Shigeo Ogawa: 94–95, 100–103
© Hitoshi Motomura: 107
© Kenta Hasegawa: 110, 120–126, 127 (top), 128–129, 131 (bottom), 132–133, 161 (right), 163 (bottom), 164–165, 167, 191–267
© Studio Basket: 114–115
© Ryo Takatsuka: 116–119
© Schemata Architects: 131 (top 8 images)
© studio-L: 140, 142, 144–147
© CHAr: 158–159, 161 (left), 162, 163 (top), 166
© VUILD: 178, 179, 181 (right)
© Hayato Kurobe: 180 (left)

Drawings, sketches, diagrams, and paintings:

Courtesy of Tsuyama City Museum: 16–17
© studio-L: 34, 136, 138
© Kumiko Inui: 38–39, 54
© Inui Architects: 42–43, 46–48
© AS: 66, 67, 74, 75, 83
© Miho Tominaga and Takahito Ito: 88, 90–91, 96, 97
© Miho Tominaga: 104–106
© Schemata Architects: 127 (bottom), 130
© studio-L: 136, 138
© Bureau of Urban Development, Tokyo Metropolitan Government: 152
© CHAr: 154, 156–157, 160, 168–169
© VUILD: 172, 182–185
© "Revitalizing Onomichi: Architecture, Community, Territory" studio, spring 2023, Harvard University Graduate School of Design: 275, 277
© Hugh Taylor: 278–281
© Ruizhu Han: 283–284

© Emily Hu: 286–287
© Yihan Liu: 288–289
© Oonagh Davis: 290–293
© Andreea Adam: 294–297
© Grace Cheng: 298–301

All other illustrations were produced by and belong to the Japan Research Initiative at the Harvard University Graduate School of Design.

Cover photo © Kenta Hasegawa, 2023

Revitalizing Japan: Architecture, Urbanization, and Degrowth

EDITORS
Mohsen Mostafavi
Kayoko Ota

TRANSLATION
Alan Gleason: Essays by Toyo Ito, Kumiko Inui, Jun Aoki, Takahito Ito and Miho Tominaga, Jo Nagasaka, Yutaro Muraji, and Koki Akiyoshi
Sam Holden: Essay by Ryo Yamazaki

JAPAN RESEARCH INITIATIVE TEAM
Wentao Guo
Grace Cheng
Nana Komoriya
Siyu Zhu

TEXT EDITING
Ophelia John
Elizabeth Kugler

COORDINATION
Thetis Li

DESIGN DIRECTION
Takumi Akin (Folder Studio)

DESIGN
Jack Burnside

COVER
Takumi Akin, Wesley Chou (Folder Studio)

This publication is part of the Japan Research Initiative at the Harvard University Graduate School of Design.

PUBLISHED BY
Actar Publishers, New York and Barcelona

DISTRIBUTION
Actar D, Inc., New York and Barcelona

New York
440 Park Avenue South, 17th Floor
New York, NY 10016, USA
T +1 212 966 2207
salesnewyork@actar-d.com

Barcelona
Roca i Batlle 2
08023 Barcelona, Spain
T +34 933 282 183
eurosales@actar-d.com

INDEXING
English ISBN: 978-1-63840-140-7
Library of Congress Control Number: 2024934323